Children's and Young Adult Literature by Native Americans:
A Guide for Librarians, Teachers, Parents, and Students

Sherry York

Published by Linworth Publishing, Inc.
480 East Wilson Bridge Road, Suite L
Worthington, Ohio, 43085

Copyright © 2003 by Linworth Publishing, Inc.

All rights reserved. Purchasing this book entitles a librarian to reproduce activity sheets for use in the library within a school or entitles a teacher to reproduce activity sheets for single classroom use within a school. Other portions of the book (up to 15 pages) may be copied for staff development purposes within a single school. Standard citation information should appear on each page. The reproduction of any part of this book for an entire school or school system or for commercial use is strictly prohibited. No part of this book may be electronically reproduced, transmitted, or recorded without written permission from the publisher.

ISBN 1-58683-119-4

Table of Contents

Introduction	**Overview**	1
	Purpose	2
	Terminology, Tribes, and Names	2
	Criteria for Inclusion	3
	Format	4
Chapter 1	**Fiction**	7
Chapter 2	**Folklore**	27
Chapter 3	**Storytelling and Drama**	41
	American Indian Storytellers	48
Chapter 4	**Poetry and Anthologies**	51
	American Indian Literature Anthologies	55
Chapter 5	**Nonfiction**	59
Chapter 6	**Resources**	81
Chapter 7	**Authors and Illustrators**	85
Appendix A	**Publishers**	103
Appendix B	**Index**	109

About the Author

Sherry York worked as an educator in Texas schools for 29 years before retiring. During her career, she taught English, language arts and reading, directed a Right to Read program, worked as a school librarian, completed an in-house automation of a library, and served on two public library boards. She conducted faculty in-service programs, served on district and regional committees, started and sponsored two student literary magazines, and reviewed books for several magazines and journals.

Since retirement she has enjoyed book reviewing, providing programs at professional conferences and book festivals, working as an editorial consultant, and writing articles and books. York and her husband Donnie, also a school librarian, divide their time between San Angelo, Texas and Ruidoso, New Mexico.

Acknowledgements

I offer my thanks to these individuals who have made this publication possible: "Cousin" Eric Gansworth, who answered my questions thoughtfully and thoroughly; Donnie York, who cleaned, cooked, did the laundry, walked the dog, AND proofread; Marlene Woo-Lun, Donna Miller, and all the crew at Linworth, who are absolutely the best people in publishing.

This book is dedicated to
Carole Haynes —
the bravest person I know.

Introduction

Overview

Librarians, teachers, parents, and students, welcome to the world of children's and young adult literature by American Indians. How many books have you read that were written by Native American authors? Unless you are a Native American or happen to live or work in an area near a population of American Indians, it is possible that you have never had any dealings with them. You may not know much about American Indian literature, histories, cultures, or peoples.

Native Americans are not all alike. They live in many geographical locations, belong to a number of distinct tribes, and have a wide variety of cultural heritages. In fact, the only way in which American Indians are alike is that their ancestors were living on the North American continent when Europeans "discovered" it.

Five centuries later in the United States we find Native Americans who have survived generations of genocide. Sadly, centuries of mistreatment are a part of the historical heritage of Native Americans in our country today. This is not to say that American Indians of today are tragic victims of history who should be pitied. Rather, we need to understand the historical backgrounds of Native Americans, African Americans, Latinos, Asian Americans, and all ethnic groups that make up our great nation.

True multicultural education promotes understanding and cooperation through the use of authentic literature. Books and educational materials authored by Native Americans can be used to overcome stereotypical thinking and educate students (who may also be parents, teachers, or librarians) about real American Indians — how they live and work, their philosophical views about life, and their history.

Books and educational materials provided in libraries and used in classrooms should be as authentic and accurate as possible. After providing authentic and accurate materials, we then need to guide students toward asking questions and finding their own answers. Students of any ethnic group and of any age will profit from exposure to these works of literature by American Indians. Learning from authentic literature means not learning stereotypes. Parents and grandparents may wish to encourage their children to learn about the variety of cultures in our country. From learning comes understanding. From understanding comes respect.

Purpose

The purpose of this guide is to help librarians, teachers, parents, and students locate books written by American Indians. It is the author's hope that readers of this guide will seek out these books and materials and enjoy reading or listening to these works of literature. Hopefully, improved access to this literature will lead to an awareness that this is literature by and about real people and that regardless of cultural background and history, we share many similarities and a few interesting differences.

Terminology, Tribes, and Names

Native Americans? American Indians? What is the proper term to use when speaking of this indigenous group? As with most complex questions, there is no simple answer. We are all people. We are all human beings, but how do we further identify these specific peoples?

"Native American" seems to be the most politically correct term. However, it has been pointed out that this term can apply to any and all persons born in this geographical area. Hence, all citizens who were born here are "native" Americans.

American? Although we in the United States call ourselves Americans, citizens of Mexico and Canada are also Americans. Geographically speaking, there is no country named America.

Indian? The term "Indian" is derived from the Spanish word "indio" used to indicate the people that a confused Christopher Columbus thought were inhabitants of India. Terms used in other parts of the world include "aborigines," "first nations," and "first peoples." Although none of these terms are exactly suitable, "Native American" and "American Indian" are used interchangeably in this guide.

Personal identity involves more than ethnicity. The author of this guide is a teacher, librarian, editor, writer, an inhabitant of Texas and New Mexico, and is of Anglo descent. These are facts. However, she has never referred to herself as an "Anglo American." Her friend Eric is a college professor, a novelist, a poet, an artist, and a member of the Onondaga tribe who grew up on the Tuscarora reservation in New York state. He does not refer to himself as a "Native American." Ethnicity is only one aspect of who we are.

For American Indians, personal identity often involves individual tribal affiliations. Indigenous peoples in the United States come from a number of tribal groups with different languages, customs, geographical locations, and histories. Some individuals have a mixed heritage with several tribal affiliations from parents and grandparents.

According to a U.S. Census fact sheet issued in 2001 for Native American Heritage month, the number of American Indians, including those from Alaska, was 2.5 million. Because the 2000 census allowed individuals to check more than one category, many persons checked combinations of races. Another census category included Native Hawaiians and Pacific Islanders. States with the largest numbers of American Indians were California, Oklahoma, Arizona, New Mexico, and Alaska. Analysis by percentages of the total populations would lead to different rankings among the states. <www.census.gov/Press-Release/www/2001/cb01fff15.html>

Native Americans as a group are not easily categorized. To complicate the situation, there are American Indians living on reservations and off reservations. There are recognized tribal units, and tribal units that have not been officially recognized by the United States government. There are Native Americans in Puerto Rico and in many states including Alaska and Hawaii. Large numbers of American Indians live in urban settings like New York, Los Angeles, and Chicago. An entire series of maps would be necessary to accurately convey the geographical locations of American Indians. Those readers who wish to acquire information about the Native American population of a particular state are urged to consult the index of this book, state reference books, and Internet Web sites.

The names of tribes vary in name and spelling for a number of reasons. To the extent possible, the author has retained individual preferences for the spelling of tribal names without attempting to standardize. Therefore, readers may note that a single tribal name is listed and spelled in a number of ways.

Some American Indians have several names. Those names may include an official name as well as a name or names given by another, given either at birth or later. Names may be in languages other than English. To the extent possible, the author has included all names associated with individual writers and illustrators.

Criteria for Inclusion

Books and materials included in this guide are in print in some format and are available for purchase at the time this guide is being written. These books and materials were written by Native American writers of the United States, including Alaska and Hawaii. A few writers of Canadian origin have been included. For the purposes of this guide, writers who identity themselves as Native Americans are considered to be so regardless of blood percentages.

Most books and materials in this guide were written and published specifically for children or teen readers. A few exceptions were made for other books that the author considers potentially useful. Within these limits, the author has attempted to include all books that met these criteria. No Native-authored books for young readers were deliberately excluded. However, it is inevitable that some books and authors were overlooked for several possible reasons including publishing schedules, lack of Library of Congress cataloging, non-listing on commercial Internet stores, availability in an electronic format only, or simply due to the author's limitations. It is hoped that this guide will be helpful to those readers seeking quality children's and young adult literature by Native American authors. Readers should remember that the author is providing information, not personally endorsing or recommending each title included herein.

Format

The resources in this guide are listed in seven chapters: Fiction, Folklore, Storytelling and Drama, Poetry, Nonfiction, Resources, and Authors and Illustrators. An appendix lists publishers. Novels, chapter books, picture books, and short stories are included in the fiction chapter. The folklore section contains picture books and longer books of folklore and legends. The storytelling and drama chapter includes books, recorded stories, and a list of storytellers. In the poetry section, readers will find books of poetry and a list of anthologies. The nonfiction section contains listings of factual books and materials on a variety of subjects. The resources chapter contains materials primarily of interest to teachers and librarians. Brief biographical sketches of authors and illustrators responsible for the children's and young adult books and materials in this guide are found in Chapter 7. Writers and artists are included regardless of ethnicity.

Relevant information for each book or item may include the the information shown in the box. Obviously, not every book or item will have all of this information. However, the author has attempted to provide relevant information to help readers select materials that will meet individual needs. Publication information includes the place, company, and date of publication. Library of Congress numbers (LC#s) are used to identify cataloging information that the Library of Congress provides for many books. The editions category provides information about the various editions in which a book may have been

Title:
Author:
Illustrator:
Publication:
Series:
LC#:
Editions:
Description:
Summary:
Subjects:
Interest Level:
Reading Level:
Tests:
Reviewed:
Lists:
Note:

Format of book or item descriptions.

published. Each edition is indicated by one or more International Standard Book Numbers (ISBNs) and information about the format: paperback, hard cover, or library binding. Also listed are recorded versions of books, audio cassettes, CDs, and video cassettes.

The book's description indicates the number of pages, whether or not the book is illustrated, and the book's size in centimeters. Descriptions may also include information about bibliographies, indexes, maps, and glossaries. Summaries may be from the Library of Congress, book publishers, or the author of this guide. Subjects are taken from the Library of Congress or as adapted by the author.

Interest levels are taken from various review sources and from the books themselves. When publishers and reviewers did not agree about the interest level, all suggested levels are listed. Children and young adults develop and mature, both physically and mentally, at very different rates. When reviewers, writers, and publishers list an interest level, they are guessing that most young readers at a certain grade level or age will likely be able to read, understand, and be interested in a particular book.

Most reading levels are based on analyses done by the producers of commercial computer-based testing programs. Reading levels are based on a formula that counts and averages the number of syllables, words, and sentences in a specified section of a book. Because writers are not computers, the reading level of most books varies from page to page and depends on which sample passages are chosen for analysis. A child's reading level may be influenced by the child's interest in a specific subject or book. Reading levels should be considered as a guess rather than an absolute indicator of whether or not a child in a specific grade will be able to read a book written at that reading level.

If tests are available for either Accelerated Reader ™ or Reading Counts ™, that information is provided. This information will be especially useful for teachers, librarians, and parents of students in schools that utilize these programs.

The reviewed category lists reviewing sources in which reviews of a book have appeared. Magazines like *The Book Report*, *Booklist*, *Horn Book*, *Kirkus*, *Library Talk*, and *School Library Journal* have published reviews of many of the books in this guide. Readers concerned with reviewers' opinions are encouraged to use library resources to locate reviews. If a book has received awards or is included on national or state recommended reading lists, those facts are noted. Internet Web sites that contain useful information are noted, but should always be checked before recommending them to others. Some lists of names of Native American authors are included in this guide. These lists are included to guide readers to other Native-authored literature and should not be considered comprehensive.

Chapter 1

Fiction

Works of fiction listed in this chapter include novels, chapter books, picture books, and short story collections.

Readers interested in the history of fiction writing by Native Americans may wish to research and learn more about American Indian pioneers in the field of fiction. Some of these early writers include S. Alice Callahan (*Wynema*, 1891), Ella Cara Deloria (*Waterlily*, 1988), John Joseph Mathews (*Sundown*, 1934), D'Arcy McNickle (*The Surrounded*, 1936), Mourning Dove (*Cogewea, the Half Blood*, 1927), John Milton Oskison (*Wild Harvest*, 1925), and John Rollin Ridge (*History of Joaquin Murieta*, 1927).

In addition to the authors included in this chapter, these are some other Native American authors of fiction:

Sherman Alexie, Paula Gunn Allen, Jeannette Armstrong, José Barreiro, Denton Bedford, Betty Louise Bell, Win Blevins, Charles Brashear, A. A. Carr, Robert J. Conley, Elizabeth Cook-Lynn, Todd Downing, Debra Magpie Earling, Keith Egawa, Jack Forbes, Eric Gansworth, Antonio Garcez, Robert Franklin Gish, Diane Glancy, Owl Goingback, Janet Campbell Hale, Geary Hobson, Linda Hogan, LeAnne Howe, Winona LaDuke, Adrian Louis, Joseph Marshall III, Mardi Oakley Medawar, Joel Monture, Beatrice Mosionier, Nasnaga, Simon J. Ortiz, Louis Owens, W. S. Penn, Robert Perea, Susan Power, Polingaysi Qoyawama, Ron Querry, Charles Red Corn, Pax Riddle, Ralph Salisbury, William Sanders, Greg Sarris, Leslie Marmon Silko, Martin Cruz Smith, Hyemeyohsts Storm, Gerald Vizenor, Anna Lee Walters, James Welch, Gerry William, Ted Williams, Shirley Hill Witt, Joan Leslie Woodruff, and Elizabeth Woody.

The Arrow over the Door

Author: Joseph Bruchac
Illustrator: James Watling
Publication: New York: Dial Books for Young Readers, 1998
LC#: 96036701
Editions: 0803720785 hc., 0141305711 pb. Puffin
Description: 89 pages, illustrated, 22 cm, 9 chapters, author's note
Summary: In the year 1777, a group of Quakers and a party of Indians have a memorable meeting.
Subjects:
Indians of North America—New York (State)—Juvenile/Fiction
Quakers—Fiction
United States—History—18th century—Fiction
Interest Level: Ages 9-12, Grades 3-7, 4-7
Reading Level: 5.2
Tests: Accelerated Reader, Reading Counts
Reviewed: *Booklist*, *Kirkus*
Lists: Oyate
Note: Told in alternating points of view of Samuel Russell, a Quaker boy, and Stands Straight, an Abenaki Indian boy.

Ashkii's Journey

Author and Illustrator: Verna Clinton
Publication: Flagstaff, AZ: Salina Bookshelf, 2001
LC#: 2001006345
Editions: 1893354318 hc.
Description: Picture book, 32 pages, illustrated
Summary: A young Navajo boy comes of age following his family's return from Bosque Redondo.
Subjects:
Coming of age—Fiction
Indians of North America—Southwest, New—Fiction
Navajo Indians—Juvenile/Fiction

Bears Make Rock Soup and Other Stories

Author: Lise Erdrich
Illustrator: Lisa Fifield
Publication: San Francisco: Children's Book Press, 2002
LC#: 2001042461
Editions: 0892391723 hc.
Description: 32 pages, color illustrations, 26 cm
Summary: A collection of stories inspired by paintings that depict the special relationships between the Plains Indians and such animals as bear, deer, moose, crows, and loons.
Subjects:
Animals—Fiction
Children's Stories, American
Indians of North America—Great Plains—Juvenile/Fiction
Short stories
Interest Level: Ages 6 and up
Note: Teacher's guide available at <www.childrensbookpress.org>

The Birchbark House

Author: Louise Erdrich
Publication: New York Hyperion Books for Children, 1999; Thorndike, ME: Thorndike Press, 2000
LC#s: 98046366 Hyperion, 99043309 Thorndike
Editions: 0786803002 hc., 078622178X hc. large print, 0786814543 pb., 1883332796 unabridged audio cassette, Audio Bookshelf, 1883332834 unabridged audio CD, Audio Bookshelf

Description: 244 pages, illustrated, 23 cm (Hyperion); 272 pages, illustrated, maps, 23 cm (Thorndike)

Summary: Omakayas, a seven-year-old Native American girl of the Ojibwa tribe, lives through the joys of summer and the perils of winter on an island in Lake Superior in 1847.

Subjects:

Indians of North America—Superior, Lake, Region—Fiction

Islands—Fiction

Ojibwa Indians—Juvenile/Fiction

Seasons—Fiction

Superior, Lake, Region—Fiction

Interest Level: Ages 9-12, 10-14, Grades 5-9

Reading Level: 6.1

Tests: Accelerated Reader, Reading Counts

Reviewed: *Booklist, Horn Book, Kirkus, New York Times, Publishers Weekly*

Lists: *Booklist* Editor's Choice 1999, California Department of Education, Georgia Children's Book Award, *Horn Book* Fanfare 2000, Kansas William Allen White Award, Maine Children's Book Award 2000-2001, *New York Times* Notable Children's Books 1999, NCSS 2000, Oyate, Pacific Northwest Young Reader's Choice Award, Tennessee Volunteer State, Vermont Dorothy Canfield Fisher 2000-2001, ALA Notable Books 2000

Note: National Book Award

The Blue Roses

Author: Linda Boyden

Illustrator: Amy Córdova

Publication: New York: Lee & Low Books, 2002

LC#: 2001038141

Editions: 158430037X lib bdg.

Description: Picture book, 32 pages, illustrated, 24 cm

Summary: A Native American girl gardens with the grandfather who helps to raise her and learns about life and loss when he dies. He then speaks to her from a dream where he is surrounded by blue roses.

Subjects:

Death—Fiction

Gardening—Fiction

Grandfathers—Fiction

Indians of North America—Fiction

Interest Level: Ages 4-8, 5-8, Grades K-3

Reviewed: *Booklist, School Library Journal*

Note: New Voices Award, Lee & Low Books

The Butterfly Dance

Author and Illustrator: Gerald Dawavendewa

Publication: Washington, D.C.: National Museum of the American Indian, Smithsonian Institution; New York: Abbeville Press, 2001

Series: *Tales of the People*

LC#: 99045051

Editions: 0789201615 hc.

Description: Picture book, 32 pages, illustrated, 25 cm

Summary: Because she is now twelve, Sihumana gets to join the other Hopi in performing the Butterfly Dance, helping to celebrate family and bring gentle rains for the flowers and plants.

Subjects:

Dance—Fiction

Hopi Indians—Juvenile/Fiction

Indian dance—Fiction

Indians of North America—Arizona—Fiction

Rain dances—Fiction

Interest Level: Ages 4-8

Reviewed: *Dallas Morning News, Horn Book, School Library Journal*

Ceremony—in the Circle of Life

Author: White Deer of Autumn
Illustrator: Daniel San Souci
Publication: Milwaukee, Wis.: Raintree Publishers, 1983; Hillsboro, OR: Beyond Words Publishing, 1991
LC#: 83007353
Editions: 0940742241 lib. bdg., 094183168X pb. (Beyond), 0613133552 lib. bdg. Econo-Clad, 0606051953 turtleback Demco
Description: Picture book, 32 pages, color illustrations, 22 cm
Summary: Nine-year-old Little Turtle, a Native American boy growing up in the city without a knowledge of his ancestors' beliefs, is visited by Star Spirit, who introduces him to the traditional teachings and rituals.
Subjects:
Indians of North America—Fiction
Indians of North America—Religion
Interest Level: Ages 9-12, Grades 2-5
Reading Level: 4.0
Tests: Reading Counts
Note: <www.beyondword.com/books/ccl.html>

Children of the Longhouse

Author: Joseph Bruchac
Publication: New York: Dial Books for Young Readers, 1996
LC#: 95011344
Editions: 0803717938, 0803717946 lib. bdg., 0140385045 pb., 0613074696 lib. bdg. Econo-Clad
Description: 150 pages, 22 cm, bibliography
Summary: Eleven-year-old Ohkwa'ri and his twin sister must make peace with a hostile gang of older boys in their Mohawk village during the late 1400s.
Subjects:
Brothers and sisters—Fiction
Indians of North America—Fiction
Mohawk Indians—Fiction
Mohawk Indians—Juvenile/Fiction
Twins—Fiction
Interest Level: Ages 9-12, Grades 3-6, 3-7
Reading Level: 5.5
Tests: Accelerated Reader, Reading Counts
Reviewed: *Booklist, Horn Book, Kirkus, Publishers Weekly, School Library Journal*
Lists: Oyate
Note: NCSA Crown Award 1999-2000

Circle of Wonder

Author: N. Scott Momaday
Publication: Santa Fe: Clear Light Publishers, 1994; Albuquerque: University of New Mexico Press, 1999
LC#s: 93005387 (Clear), 99030353 (UNM)
Editions: 0940666324 (Clear), 0826321496 hc. (UNM), 0826327974 audio cassette (UNM)
Description: 40 pages, color illustrations, 26 cm
Summary: A mute Indian child has an extraordinary experience one Christmas when he follows a figure who seems to be his beloved dead grandfather and he becomes part of a circle in which he, animals, nature, and all the world join in a moment of peace and goodwill.
Subjects:
Christmas—Fiction
Grandfathers—Fiction
Indians of North America—New Mexico—Juvenile/Fiction
Mutism—Fiction
New Mexico—Fiction
Interest Level: Ages 9-12
Reviewed: *Bloomsbury Review*

Cloudwalker: Contemporary Native American Stories

Author: Joel Monture
Illustrator: Carson Waterman
Publication: Golden, CO: Fulcrum Publishing, 1996
LC#: 95042815
Editions: 1555912257 hc.
Description: Short stories, 64 pages, illustrated, 24 cm, glossary, 6 stories
Subjects:
Children's stories, American
Indians of North American—Juvenile/Fiction
Short stories
Interest Level: Ages 9-12
Reading Level: 5.3
Tests: Accelerated Reader
Reviewed: *Horn Book*
Lists: Oyate
Note: Short stories by American Indian children.

Crazy Horse's Vision

Author: Joseph Bruchac
Illustrator: S. D. Nelson
Publication: New York: Lee & Low Books, 2000
LC#: 99047451
Editions: 1880000946 hc.
Description: Picture book, 40 pages, color illustrations, 28 cm, author's note, illustrator's note
Summary: A story based on the life of the dedicated young Lakota boy who grew up to be one of the bravest defenders of his people.
Subjects:
Crazy Horse, ca. 1842-1877—Fiction
Indians of North America—Great Plains—Fiction
Oglala Indians—Fiction
Interest Level: Grades 1-5, 2-4
Reading Level: 4.0
Tests: Accelerated Reader, Reading Counts
Reviewed: *Booklist*, *Horn Book*, *Kirkus*, *Publishers Weekly*, *School Library Journal*, *Teaching Tolerance*
Lists: ALA Notable Books 2001, Notable NCSS, Oyate, Prairie Pasque Children's Book list South Dakota Library Association 2002-2003, Sequoyah Children's Book list Oklahoma Library Association 2002-2003, Teachers' Choice 2001 International Reading Association
Note: <www.leeandlow.com/books/vision.html>
Note: Parent's Choice Gold Award 2000

Did You Hear Wind Sing Your Name? An Oneida Song of Spring

Author: Sandra De Coteau Orie
Illustrator: Christopher Canyon
Publication: New York: Walker, 1995
LC#: 94031102
Editions: 0802783503 hc., 0802783511 lib. bdg., 0802774857 pb.
Description: Picture book, 32 pages, color illustrations, 22 × 28 cm
Summary: Pictures and words pay homage to the Oneida Indians' view of the cycle of spring.
Subjects:
Indians of North America—Fiction
Nature—Fiction

Oneida Indians—Fiction

Spring—Fiction

Interest Level: Ages 4-8, Grades P-2

Reading Level: 2.0

Reviewed: *Horn Book, Midwest Book Review*

Lists: Maryland Children's Book Award, Oyate

Dog People: Native Dog Stories

Author: Joseph Bruchac

Illustrator: Murv Jacob

Publication: Golden, CO: Fulcrum Publishing, 1995

LC#: 95009804

Editions: 1555912281 hc.

Description: Short stories, 64 pages, illustrated, 24 cm, glossary, 6 stories

Summary: A series of stories, set in the northern New England ten thousand years ago, about the special relationship between the Abenaki people and the dogs who were their faithful friends.

Subjects:

Abenaki Indians—Juvenile/Fiction

Children's stories, American

Dogs—Fiction

Indians of North America—Fiction

Short stories

Interest Level: Ages 9-12, Grades 3-7

Reading Level: 5.4

Tests: Accelerated Reader, Reading Counts

Reviewed: *Horn Book, Midwest Book Review, School Library Journal*

Dream Feather

Author and Illustrator: Viento Stan Padilla

Publication: Summertown, TN: Book Publishing Company, 1980, 1987

LC#: 87017823

Editions: 0913990574 pb.

Description: 50 pages, illustrated, 22 cm

Summary: Guided by the wisdom within the Grandfather's words, a young boy follows the Dream Feather from the quiet of night to the awakening that radiates from the other side of the sun.

Subjects:

Indians of North America—Fiction

Interest Level: Ages 9-12

Eagle Song

Author: Joseph Bruchac

Illustrator: Dan Andreasen

Publication: New York: Dial Books for Young Readers, 1997

LC#: 95052861

Editions: 0803719183 hc., 0803719191 lib. bdg., 0141301694 pb. Puffin, 0613177908 lib. bdg. Econo-Clad

Description: 80 pages, illustrated (black and white), 23 cm, 8 chapters

Summary: After moving from a Mohawk reservation to Brooklyn, New York, eight-year-old Danny Bigtree encounters stereotypes about his Native American heritage.

Subjects:

Indians of North America—Fiction

Mohawk Indians—Juvenile/Fiction

Moving, Household—Fiction

Prejudices—Fiction

Schools—Fiction

Interest Level: Ages 9-12, Grades 2-4, 2-5

Reading Level: 3.0

Tests: Accelerated Reader, Reading Counts

Reviewed: *Booklist, Horn Book, Kirkus, Publishers Weekly, School Library Journal*

Lists: Oyate, Notable Children's Trade Books, Florida Sunshine State Young Readers Award 1999-2000

Father's Boots

Navajo title: Azhé'é bikénidoots'osii
Author: Baje Whitethorne, Sr.
Translator: Darlene Redhair
Publication: Flagstaff, AZ: Salina Bookshelf, 2001
LC#: 2001049778
Editions: 1893354296 hc.
Description: 42 pages, color illustrations, 24 cm
Summary: In this story, told in both English and Navajo, three Navajo brothers learn from their grandmother's stories about the creation of the Earth.
Subjects:
Brothers—Fiction
Grandmothers—Fiction
Indians of North America—Southwest, New—Fiction
Navajo Indians—Juvenile/Fiction
Navajo language materials—Bilingual
Storytelling—Fiction
Note: Bilingual—English and Navajo

Firedancers

Author: Jan Bourdeau
Illustrator: C. J. Taylor
Publication: Toronto, New York: Stoddard Kids, 2000
LC#: 00340572
Editions: 0773731385 hc.
Description: Picture book, 32 pages, color illustrations, 29 cm
Summary: A young Ojibwa girl and her grandmother take a night trip to Smooth Rock Island.
Subjects:
Grandmothers—Fiction
Indians of North America—Canada—Fiction
Old age—Fiction
Interest Level: Ages 4-8
Reviewed: *Booklist*

The Give-Away: A Christmas Story

Author and Illustrator: Ray Buckley
Publication: Nashville, TN: Abingdon Press, 1999
LC#: none
Editions: 0687071860 hc.
Description: Picture book, 32 pages, illustrated, 24 cm
Summary: *The Give-Away* relates a dialogue between the Whooping Crane, the Snow Goose, Old Beaver, Grandmother Turtle, the Wind, the Ancient One, the Creator, and others before the birth of Jesus.
Subjects:
Christmas—Fiction
Indians of North America—Fiction
Interest Level: Ages 4-8

The Goat in the Rug

Authors: Charles L. Blood and Martin Link
Illustrator: Nancy Winslow Parker
Publication: New York: *Parents' Magazine*, 1976; Four Winds, 1980; Atheneum, 1988; Aladdin, 1990
LC#s: 75019192 (Parents), 89077701 (Four), 89077701 (Aladdin)
Editions: 0027109208 lib. bdg. (Atheneum), 0819308285 lib. bdg. (Parents), 0833559540 lib. bdg. (Econo-Clad), 0819308277 hc. (Parents), 05990077635 hc. (Four), 06/9714181 pb. (Aladdin)

Description: 32 pages, color illustrations, 26 cm

Summary: Geraldine, a goat, describes each step as she and her Navajo friend make a rug, from the hair clippings and carding to the dyeing and actual weaving.

Subjects:

Hand weaving—Fiction

Indian textile fabrics—Southwest, New—Fiction

Hand weaving—Fiction

Navajo textile fabrics—Juvenile/Fiction

Rugs—Fiction

Interest Level: Ages 4-8, Grades 1-3, 3-7

Reading Level: 6.0

Tests: Reading Counts

Reviewed: *Booklist, Horn Book, Publishers Weekly, School Library Journal*

Lists: Reading Rainbow

Note: www.sdcoe.k12.ca.us/score/goat/goattg.html

Note: www.mcps.k12.md.us/curriculum/socialstd/grade3/Goat_Rug.html

Note: http://ecedweb.unomaha.edu/lit-goat.htm

The Good Luck Cat

Author: Joy Harjo

Illustrator: Paul Lee

Publication: San Diego, CA: Harcourt, 2000

LC#: 98017232

Editions: 0152321977 lib. bdg.

Description: Picture book, 32 pages, color illustrations, 22 × 28 cm

Summary: Because her good luck cat, Woogie, has already used up eight of his nine lives in narrow escapes from disaster, a Native American girl worries when he disappears.

Subjects:

Cats—Fiction

Indians of North America—Fiction

Luck—Fiction

Interest Level: Ages 4-8, 5-7, Grades K-3

Reading Level: 3.3

Tests: Accelerated Reader

Lists: Fifty Multicultural Books Every Child Should Know from Cooperative Children's Book Center, Oyate

Note: Charlotte Zolotow Award 2001, Highly Commended

The Great Change

Author: White Deer of Autumn

Illustrator: Carol Grigg

Publication: Hillsboro, Oregon: Beyond Words Publishing, 1992

LC#: 92014501

Editions: 0941831795 hc.

Description: Picture book, 32 pages, illustrated, 30 cm

Summary: A Native American grandmother explains the meaning of death, or the Great Change, to her questioning granddaughter.

Subjects:

Death—Fiction

Indians of North America—Fiction

Interest Level: Ages 4-8, 9-12

Reviewed: *Horn Book*

Note: <www.beyondword.com/books/gc.html>

Great Eagle and Small One

Author: Ralph Moisa, Jr.

Illustrator: Randy Messer

Publication: Logan, Iowa: Perfection Learning, 1997

Series: *Cover-to-Cover* Books

LC#: 98205842

Editions: 0780766857 hc., 0789120003 pb.

Description: 54 pages, illustrated, 23 cm, 7 chapters

Summary: In this original Yaqui legend, Great Eagle learns that needing help is sometimes part of life and that pride can make life lonely, and short. Information about the great eagle is provided.

Subjects:

Eagles—Fiction

Golden eagle—Fiction

People with disabilities—Fiction

Interest Level: Ages 9-12, Grades 2-6

Reading Level: 1.8

Green Snake Ceremony

Author: Sherrin Watkins

Illustrator: Kim Doner

Publication: Tulsa, OK: Council Oak Books, 1995

Series: *Greyfeather* series

LC#: 95037924

Editions: 0933031890 hc., 1571780572 pb.

Description: Picture book, 36 pages, color illustrations, 23 × 28 cm

Summary: As a young girl and her grandfather try to find the right kind of snake for a special Shawnee ceremony; illustrations show what a nearby green snake thinks about everything.

Subjects:

Grandparents—Fiction

Indians of North America—Oklahoma—Fiction

Shawnee Indians—Rites and ceremonies—Juvenile/Fiction

Interest Level: Ages 4-8

Reviewed: *Horn Book, School Library Journal*

Note: Gamma State Author's Award, Oklahoma Book Award

Note: Green snake book markers are included.

Guests

Author: Michael Dorris

Publication: New York: Hyperion Books for Children, 1994

LC#: 94026057

Editions: 078680047X hc., 0786820365 lib. bdg., 0786813563 pb., 0613001699 lib. bdg. Econo-Clad

Description: 128 pages, 22 cm, 8 chapters

Summary: Moss and Trouble, an Algonquin boy and girl, struggle with the problems of growing up in the Massachusetts area during the time of the first Thanksgiving.

Subjects:

Algonquian Indians—Juvenile/Fiction

America—Discovery and exploration—English—Fiction

Indians of North America—Fiction

Interest Level: Ages 9-12, Grades 3-7, 4-7

Reading Level: 5.2

Tests: Accelerated Reader, Reading Counts

Reviewed: *Booklist, Horn Book, Kirkus, Midwest Book Review, School Library Journal*

Lists: ALA Notables, California Department of Education, William Allen White Kansas, Golden Sower Nebraska

Note: Literature guide is available from Scholastic, 059006570X.

The Heart of a Chief: A Novel

Author: Joseph Bruchac

Publication: New York: Dial Books for Young Readers, 1998

LC#: 97049248

Editions: 0803722761 hc., 014131236X pb.

Description: 153 pages, 22 cm

Summary: An eleven-year-old Pennacook Indian boy living on a reservation faces his father's alcoholism, a controversy surrounding plans for a casino on a tribal island, and insensitivity toward Native Americans in his school and nearby town.

Subjects:

Alcoholism—Fiction

Indian reservations—Fiction

Indians of North America—New Hampshire—Fiction

Pennacook Indians—Fiction

Interest Level: Ages 8-12, 9-12, Grades 5-8, 5-9

Reading Level: 4.7, 6

Tests: Accelerated Reader, Reading Counts

Reviewed: *Booklist, Horn Book, Publishers Weekly, School Library Journal*

Lists: Iowa Children's Choice, Arkansas Diamond Charlie May Simon

Note: Jane Addams Children's Book Award Honor Book 1999

High Elk's Treasure (with Related Readings)

Author: Virginia Driving Hawk Sneve

Illustrator: Oren Lyons (Holiday House)

Publication: New York: Holiday House, 1972, Saint Paul, MN: EMC/Paradigm Publications, 2002

Series: *The EMC Masterpiece Series Access Editions*

LC#s: 72075600 (Holiday), 2001055673 (EMC)

Editions: 0823402126 (Holiday), 0821924141 (EMC)

Description: 110 pages, illustrated, 23 cm, map

Summary: Trying to locate a valuable filly lost during a storm, thirteen-year-old Joe High Elk discovers an object of historical importance.

Subjects:

Dakota Indians—Juvenile/Fiction

Indians of North America—Fiction

Interest Level: Ages 9-12

Note: Includes plot analysis, related readings, activities, and projects.

Indian Shoes

Author: Cynthia Leitich Smith

Illustrator: Jim Madsen

Publication: New York: HarperCollins, 2002

LC#: 2001039510

Editions: 0060295317 hc., 0060295325 lib. bdg.

Description: Short stories, 66 pages, illustrated, 22 cm, 6 stories

Summary: Together with his grandfather, Ray Halfmoon, a Seminole-Cherokee boy, finds creative and amusing solutions to life's challenges.

Subjects:

Grandfathers—Fiction

Indians of North America—Fiction

Interest Level: Ages 7-9, 9-12, Grades 3-5, 3-6

Reviewed: *Booklist, Kirkus, Publishers Weekly, School Library Journal*

Note: <www.cynthialeitichsmith.com/miindianshoes.htm>

Jingle Dancer

Author: Cynthia Leitich Smith

Illustrators: Cornelius Van Wright and Ying-Hwa Hu

Publication: New York: Morrow Junior Books, 2000

LC#: 99015503

Editions: 068816241X hc., 0688162428 lib. bdg.

Description: Picture book, 32 pages, color illustrations, 29 cm, glossary

Summary: Jenna, a member of the Muscogee, or Creek Nation, borrows jingles from the dresses of several friends and relatives so she can perform the jingle dance at the powwow. Includes a note about the jingle dance tradition and its regalia.

Subjects:

Creek Indians—Juvenile/Fiction

Dance—Fiction

Indian dance—Fiction

Indians of North America—Oklahoma—Fiction

Interest Level: Ages 4-8, Grades K-3

Reading Level: 3.7

Tests: Accelerated Reader

Reviewed: *Booklist*, *Kirkus*, *Publishers Weekly*, *School Library Journal*

Lists: Notable Children's Trade Book in the Field of Social Studies 2001, Oyate, Texas 2 by 2

Note: <www.cynthialeitichsmith.com/jingledancer.htm>

The Journal of Jesse Smoke: A Cherokee Boy

Author: Joseph Bruchac

Publication: New York: Scholastic, 2001

Series: *My Name Is America, A Dear America Book*

LC#: 00055619

Editions: 0439121973 hc.

Description: 203 pages, illustrated, 20 cm, map

Summary: Jesse Smoke, a sixteen-year-old Cherokee, begins a journal in 1837 to record the stories of his people and their difficulties as they face removal along the Trail of Tears. Includes a historical note giving details of the removal.

Subjects:

Cherokee Indians—History—Juvenile/Fiction

Diaries—Fiction

Indians of North America—Southern states—History Fiction

Trail of Tears, 1838—Juvenile/Fiction

Interest Level: Ages 9-12, Grades 3-7, 5-8

Reading Level: 6.2

Tests: Accelerated Reader, Reading Counts

Reviewed: *Booklist*

Note: <www.scholastic.com/titles/mynameisamerica/timeline/jessesmoke.htm>

Lessons from Mother Earth

Author: Elaine McLeod

Illustrator: Colleen Wood

Publication: Buffalo: Groundwood/Douglas & McIntyre, 2002

Editions: 0888993129 hc.

Description: Picture book, 24 pages, color illustrations, 23 cm

Summary: Tess visits her grandmother's garden and learns how to care for plants in the garden and in nature.

Subjects:

Grandmothers—Fiction

Nature—Fiction

Plants—Fiction

Interest Level: Ages Baby-Preschool, 4-8

Reviewed: *School Library Journal*

Limu the Blue Turtle

Author: Kimo Armitage

Illustrator: Scott Kaneshiro

Publication: Waipahu, HI: Island Heritage Publishing, 1998

Series: *Little Rainbow Books*

Editions: 0896103544 hc.

Description: Picture book, 28 pages, color illustrations, 24 cm

Summary: Although Limu is laughed at because of his outward appearance, his friends like him because he is a good turtle on the inside.
Subjects:
Friends—Fiction
Sea life—Fiction
Sea turtles—Fiction
Interest Level: Ages 4-8

Little Fish

Author: Ralph Moisa, Jr.
Illustrator: Dea Marks
Publication: Logan, IA: Perfection Learning, 1997
Series: *Cover-to-Cover Books*
LC#: 98207752
Editions: 0780766911 hc., 0789120038 pb.
Description: 56 pages, illustrated, 23 cm, 9 chapters
Summary: In this original Yaqui legend, Little Fish learns never to give up. Last two chapters contain non-fiction information about trout.
Subjects:
Fishes—Fiction
Trout—Fiction
Interest Level: Grades 2-6
Reading Level: 1.5

Longwalker's Journey: A Novel of the Choctaw Trail of Tears

Author: Beatrice O. Harrell
Illustrator: Tony Meers
Publication: New York: Dial Books for Young Readers, 1999
LC#: 98009754
Editions: 0803723806 pb.
Description: 144 pages, illustrated, 22 cm, map
Summary: When the government removes their tribe from their sacred homeland in 1831, ten-year-old Minko and his father endure terrible hardships on their journey from Mississippi to Oklahoma, where Minko receives the name Longwalker.
Subjects:
Choctaw Indians—Fiction
Frontier and pioneer life—Fiction
Indians of North America—Fiction
Longwalker—Juvenile/Fiction
Interest Level: Ages 9-12
Reading Level: 5.4
Tests: Accelerated Reader
Reviewed: *Horn Book*, *Kirkus*
Lists: ALA Booklist, Notable Books for a Global Society 2000

Mahalo e Grandpa

Author: Kimo Armitage
Illustrator: Scott Kaneshiro
Publication: Waipahu, HI: Island Heritage Publishing, 2002
Series: *Little Rainbow Books*
Editions: 0896103951 hc.
Description: Picture book, 24 pages, color illustrations, 24 cm
Summary: Kekoa's grandfather teaches him about life in Hawaii and the knowledge is passed on to his son Kaipo and to future generations.
Subjects:
Conduct of life—Fiction
Family—Fiction
Grandfathers—Fiction
Hawaii—Fiction
Hawaii—Social life and customs
Interest Level: Ages 4-8

A Man Called Raven

Author: Richard Van Camp
Illustrator: George Littlechild
Publication: San Francisco, CA: Children's Book Press, 1997
LC#: 96031905
Editions: 0892391448 lib. bdg., 0516205463 lib. bdg.
Description: Picture book, 32 pages, color illustrations, 28 cm
Summary: A mysterious man tells two Indian brothers why they must not hurt the ravens that pester them.
Subjects:
Indians of North America—Fiction
Métis—Juvenile/Fiction
Ravens—Fiction
Interest Level: Ages 4-8, 6 and up
Reviewed: *Horn Book, Kirkus, Midwest Book Reviews, School Library Journal*
Note: <www.cbookpress.org/ob/raven.html>

Manuli'i & the Colorful Cape

Author: Kimo Armitage
Illustrator: Scott Kaneshiro
Publication: Aiea, HI: Island Heritage Publishing, 2001
Series: *Little Rainbow Books*
Editions: 0896104230 hc.
Description: Picture book, 28 pages, color illustrations, 24 cm
Summary: A boy named Kaipo saves a baby bird and is rewarded because "friends take care of friends."
Subjects:
Birds—Fiction
Friends—Fiction
Hawaii—Fiction
Interest Level: Ages 4-8

Morning Girl

Author: Michael Dorris
Publication: New York: Hyperion Books for Children, 1992
LC#: 92052989
Editions: 1562822845 hc., 1562822853 lib. bdg., 078681358X pb., 0786813725 pb., 0785738452 lib. bdg. Econo-Clad
Description: 80 pages, 22 cm, 9 chapters plus epilogue, historical fiction
Summary: Morning Girl, who loves the day, and her younger brother Star Boy, who loves the night, take turns describing their life on an island in pre-Columbian America; in Morning Girl's last narrative, she witnesses the arrival of the first Europeans to her world.
Subjects:
America—Discovery and exploration—Spanish—Fiction
Arawak Indians—Juvenile/Fiction
Brothers and sisters—Fiction
Indians of the West Indies—Fiction
Interest Level: Ages 7-12, 9-12
Reading Level: 4.9
Tests: Accelerated Reader, Reading Counts
Reviewed: *Horn Book, Kirkus, Kliatt, Publishers Weekly*
Lists: H. W. Wilson's Children's Catalog, *School Library Journal* Best Book, *NY Times* Book Review Notable, Booklist Editor's Choice, *Publishers Weekly* Best Book of the Year, *Horn Book* Fanfare Book, California Department of Education, Green Bay Public Schools
Note: <www.wmich.edu/dialogues/texts/morninggirl.html>
Note: Scott O'Dell Award

Morning on the Lake

Author: Jan Bourdeau Waboose
Illustrator: Karen Reczuch

Publication: Buffalo, NY: Kids Can Press, 1997

Editions: 1550743732 hc., 1550745883 pb.

Description: Picture book, 32 pages, illustrated, 24 cm

Summary: Noshen and his grandfather take a canoe trip, climb a cliff, and walk through the woods at night.

Subjects:

Grandfathers—Fiction

Indians of North America—Fiction

Ojibwa Indians—Fiction

Interest Level: Ages 5-9

Reading Level: 3.7

Tests: Accelerated Reader, Reading Counts

Reviewed: *Booklist*, *Kirkus*

Lists: Fifty Multicultural Books Every Child Should Know, Cooperative Children's Book Center, OLA (Ontario Library Association) Best Bets 1997, Oyate

My Name is Seepeetza

Author: Shirley Sterling

Publication: Buffalo: Groundwood/Douglas & McIntyre, 1992

LC#: 93202302

Editions: 0888991657 pb., 0888992904 hc., 061334868 lib. bdg. Econo-Clad

Description: 126 pages, 29 cm, bildungsromane, diary fiction, a series of journal entries—not divided into chapters

Summary: When Seepeetza is six years old, she is forced to leave her parents' ranch and her family to live at the Kalamak Indian Residential School.

Subjects:

Canada—Fiction

Girls—Fiction

Salish Indians—Fiction

Interest Level: Ages 9-12, 10-12, Grades 3-7, 5-10

Reading Level: 4.8

Tests: Accelerated Reader

Reviewed: *Booklist*, *Horn Book*, *Publishers Weekly*

Lists: California Department of Education, Oyate

Note: <www.sd23.bc.ca/cotla/bookcase/seepeetza.html>

Note: Sheila A. Egoff Children's Book Prize

Owl in the Cedar Tree

Author: Natachee Scott Momaday

Illustrator: Don Perceval

Publication: Boston: Ginn, 1965; Lincoln: University of Nebraska Press, 1992

LC#s: 65025051 (Ginn), 91041866 (UN Press)

Editions: 0803281846 pb., U. Nebraska

Description: 114 pages, illustrated, 22 cm, 17 chapters

Summary: A Navajo boy with a secret wish is torn by conflicting cultures.

Subjects:

Indians of North America—Fiction

Navajo Indians—Juvenile/Fiction

Interest Level: Ages 9-12

Reviewed: *Booklist*, *Library Journal*

Rain Is Not My Indian Name

Author: Cynthia Leitich Smith

Publication: New York: HarperCollins, 2001

LC#: 00059705

Editions: 0688173977 hc., 006029504X lib. bdg., 0807204293 unabridged audio cassette (Bantam)

Description: 135 pages, 22 cm

Summary: Tired of staying in seclusion since the death of her best friend, a fourteen-year-old Native American girl takes on a photographic assignment with her local newspaper to cover events at the Native American summer youth camp.

Subjects:

Death—Fiction

Grief—Fiction

Indians of North America—Fiction

Photography—Fiction

Interest Level: Ages 9-12, 10-14, Grades 6-10

Reading Level: 5.8

Tests: Accelerated Reader

Reviewed: *Bulletin of the Center for Children's Books, Kirkus, Publishers Weekly, School Library Journal, VOYA*

Lists: Oyate

Note: <www.cynthialeitichsmith.com/rainisnotmyindianname.html>

Runner in the Sun: A Story of Indian Maize

Author: D'Arcy McNickle

Illustrator: Allan C. Houser

Publication: Albuquerque: University of New Mexico Press, 1982, 1987

Series: *A Zia book*

LC#: 87005986

Editions: 0826309747 pb., 0030350603 lib. bdg. Holt

Description: 259 pages, illustrated, 21 cm

Summary: A story of pre-Hispanic Indian life in the area that is now the American Southwest.

Subjects:

Indians of North America—Southwest, New—Juvenile/Fiction

Interest Level: Ages 4-8

Sacajawea: The Story of Bird Woman and the Lewis and Clark Expedition

Author: Joseph Bruchac

Publication: San Diego, CA: Silver Whistle/Harcourt, 2000

LC#: 99047653

Editions: 0152022341 lib. bdg., 0439280680 pb. Scholastic, 0613443683 lib. bdg. Econo-Clad

Description: 200 pages, 22 cm, maps, bibliography, 35 chapters, historical fiction

Summary: Sacajawea, a Shoshone Indian interpreter, peacemaker, and guide, and William Clark alternate in describing their experiences on the Lewis and Clark Expedition to the Northwest.

Subjects:

Clark, William, 1770-1838—Juvenile/Fiction

Indians of North America—Fiction

Lewis and Clark Expedition (1804-1806)—Juvenile/Fiction

Sacajawea, 1786-1884—Juvenile/Fiction

Interest Level: Ages 12 and up, Grades 5-8, 7-12, young adult

Reading Level: 5.7

Tests: Accelerated Reader, Reading Counts

Reviewed: *Booklist, Kirkus*

Lists: Lamplighter Award 2002-2003, North Carolina Battle of the Books, Notable Social Studies Trade Book 2001, 100 of the Decade's Best Multicultural Read-Alouds, Philadelphia School District Recommended Reading, Reading Is Fundamental

Note: <www.secondaryenglish.com/sacajawea.html>

The Secret of Dead Man's Mine: A Rinnah Two Feathers Mystery

Author: Rodney Johnson
Illustrator: Jill Thompson
Publication: Los Angeles: UglyTown, 2001
LC#: 00012929
Editions: 0966347331 pb.
Description: 248 pages, illustrated, 18 cm, 19 chapters
Summary: Rinnah Two Feathers, a sleuth-minded Lakota Indian in South Dakota, investigates a mysterious stranger poking around a long-abandoned house and stumbles across the secret of Dead Man's Mine.
Subjects:
Indians of North America—North Dakota—Fiction
Mystery and detective stories
North Dakota—Fiction
Teton Indians—Juvenile/Fiction
Interest Level: Ages 9-12, Grades 5-7
Reviewed: *School Library Journal*
Reviewed: <http://reviewlutions.hikeeba.com/reviews/deadmansmine.html>
Note: Includes a recipe for fry bread.
Note: The sequel is *Curse of the Royal Ruby* (UglyTown, November 2002).

Sees Behind Trees

Author: Michael Dorris
Publication: New York: Hyperion Books for Children, 1996
LC#: 96015859
Editions: 0786802243 hc., 0786822155 lib. bdg., 0786813571 pb., 061305850X lib. bdg. Econo-Clad
Description: 104 pages, 22 cm, 9 chapters
Summary: A Native American boy with a special gift to "see" beyond his poor eyesight journeys with an old warrior to a land of mystery and beauty.
Subjects:
Blind—Fiction
Indians of North America—Juvenile/Fiction
Physically handicapped—Fiction
Interest Level: Ages 9-12, Grades 3-6, 3-7
Reading Level: 5.2
Tests: Accelerated Reader, Reading Counts
Reviewed: *Booklist*, *Horn Book*, *Kirkus*, *New York Times*, *Publishers Weekly*, *School Library Journal*
Lists: Alabama Emphasis on Reading, Capitol Choices, Florida Sunshine, Great Stone Face Children's Book Award, H. W. Wilson's *Children's Catalog*, Indiana Read-Aloud, Maine Student Book Award, Maryland Black-Eyed Susan Book Award, Texas Bluebonnet, Texas Lone Star, Virginia Young Reader, Wyoming Indian Paintbrush
Note: <www.angelfire.com/mn2/APS/nativeamerican/story1.html>

Skeleton Man

Author: Joseph Bruchac
Publication: New York: HarperCollins Publishers, 2001
LC#: 00054345
Editions: 0060290757 hc., 0060290765 lib. bdg.
Description: 128 pages, 20 cm, 16 chapters
Summary: After her parents disappear and she is turned over to the care of a strange "great-uncle," Molly must rely on her dreams about an old Mohawk story for her safety and maybe even for her life.
Subjects:
Indians of North America—New York (State)—Fiction
Kidnapping—Fiction
Mohawk Indians—Fiction

Psychopaths—Fiction

Interest Level: Ages 9-12, Grades 4-7, 5-9

Reading Level: 4.8, 6

Tests: Accelerated Reader

Reviewed: *Booklist, Bulletin for the Center for Children's Books, Kirkus, Publishers Weekly, School Library Journal*

Lists: ALA Notable Books 2000, Children's Choices 2002, *School Library Journal's* Best Books 2001, Texas Lone Star

SkySisters

Author: Jan Bourdeau Waboose

Illustrator: Brian Deines

Publication: Toronto, Niagara Falls, NY: Kids Can Press, 2000

LC#: 2001320732

Editions: 1550746979 hc., 1550746995 pb.

Description: Picture book, 32 pages, color illustrations, 24 × 27 cm

Summary: Two Ojibwa sisters set off across the frozen north country to see the Sky Spirit's midnight dance.

Subjects:

Auroras—Fiction

Indians of North America—Fiction

Ojibwa Indians—Fiction

Sisters—Fiction

Interest Level: Ages 3-7, Ages 4-8, Grades K-3

Reading Level: 3.1

Tests: Accelerated Reader

Reviewed: *Booklist, Horn Book, School Library Journal*

Lists: Oyate

Note: Skipping Stones Honor Award 2001

Spirit of the White Bison

Author: Beatrice Culleton Mosionier

Illustrator: Robert Kakaygeesick, Jr.

Publication: Summertown, TN: Book Publishing Co., 1989. Originally published in Canada by Pemmican Publications, Inc.

LC#: 89032047

Editions: 0913990647 pb.

Description: 64 pages, illustrated, 23 cm

Subjects:

American bison—Fiction

Indians of North America—Fiction

Interest Level: Ages 9-12

Squanto's Journey: The Story of the First Thanksgiving

Author: Joseph Bruchac

Illustrator: Greg Shed

Publication: San Diego: Silver Whistle/Harcourt, 2000

LC#: 99012012

Editions: 0152018174 lib. bdg. (Silver), 0739830724 lib. bdg. (Raintree)

Description: Picture book, 32 pages, color illustrations, 23 × 28 cm, glossary, author's note

Summary: Squanto recounts how he was captured by the British in 1614, sold into slavery in Spain, and ultimately returned to the New World to become a guide and friend for the colonists.

Subjects:

Indians of North America—Massachusetts—Fiction

Pilgrims (New Plymouth Colony)—Fiction

Squanto—Juvenile/Fiction

Wampanoag Indians—Juvenile/Fiction

Interest Level: Ages 4-8, 6-9, Grades 1-5

Reading Level: 4.2
Tests: Accelerated Reader, Reading Counts
Lists: Notable Social Studies Trade Books 2001

Sunpainters: Eclipse of the Navajo Sun

Author and Illustrator: Baje Whitethorne
Publication: Flagstaff, AZ: Northland, 1994; Flagstaff, AZ: Salina Bookshelf, 2002
LC#: 94011146 (Northland), 2001008558 (Salina)
Editions: 0873585879 hc. (Northland), 1893354334 hc. (Salina)
Description: Picture book, 32 pages, color illustrations, 1994
Summary: Explaining a solar eclipse, a Navajo tells his grandson that when the sun dies the children of Mother Earth are called from the four directions to repaint the universe in all the colors of the rainbow.
Subjects:
Folklore—United States
Grandfathers—Fiction
Indians of North America—Folklore
Indians of North America—Southwest, New—Fiction
Navajo Indians—Fiction
Navajo Indians—Folklore
Solar eclipses—Fiction
Solar eclipses—Folklore
Reviewed: *Horn Book*
Lists: Oyate

What's the Most Beautiful Thing You Know about Horses?

Author: Richard Van Camp
Illustrator: George Littlechild
Publication: San Francisco, CA: Children's Book Press, 1998
LC#: 97037437
Editions: 0892391545 hc., 0516216481 lib. bdg.
Description: Picture book, 32 pages, color illustrations, 28 cm
Summary: On the coldest day of the year in a small community in the Northwest Territories, a stranger to horses searches among family and friends for the answer to an important question.
Subjects:
Horses—Fiction
Indians of North America—Canada—Fiction
Métis—Fiction
Northwest Territories—Fiction
Questions and answers—Fiction
Interest Level: Ages 4-8, 6-8
Reviewed: *Horn Book, Kirkus*

When Thunders Spoke

Author: Virginia Driving Hawk Sneve
Illustrator: Oren Lyons
Publication: New York: Holiday House, 1974; Lincoln: University of Nebraska Press, 1993
LC#s: 73078453 (Holiday), 93010953 (University)
Editions: 0823402304 lib. bdg., (Holiday), 0803292201 pb. University
Description: 95 pages, illustrated, 21 cm, glossary, 7 chapters

Summary: After a fifteen-year-old Sioux boy finds a sacred stick, unusual things begin to happen to his family.

Subjects:

Dakota Indians—Juvenile/Fiction

Indians of North America—Fiction

Interest Level: Ages 9-12

Lists: Oyate

White Bead Ceremony

Author: Sherrin Watkins

Illustrator: Kim Doner

Publication: Tulsa, OK: Council Oak Books, 1994

Series: *Greyfeather* series

LC#: 93050735

Editions: 0933031920 hc., 0933031262 hc., 1571780564 pb.

Description: Picture book, 40 pages, color illustrations, 22 × 29 cm

Summary: Mary Greyfeather experiences the traditional Shawnee ceremony by which children are given a tribal name.

Subjects:

Indians of North America—Rites and ceremonies—Fiction

Shawnee Indians—Rites and ceremonies—Juvenile/Fiction

Interest Level: Ages 4-8

Reviewed: *Horn Book*

Note: Includes language cards.

Note: Includes a one-page Shawnee history.

The Window

Author: Michael Dorris

Publication: New York: Hyperion Books for Children, 1997

LC#: 97002822

Editions: 078603010 hc., 0786822406 lib. bdg., 0786813172 pb., 0786813733 pb., 061318291X lib. bdg. Econo-Clad

Description: 112 pages, 19 cm

Summary: When ten-year-old Rayona's Native American mother enters a treatment facility, her estranged father, a black man, finally introduces her to his side of the family, who are not at all what she expected.

Subjects:

Family—Fiction

Parent and child—Fiction

Racially mixed people—Fiction

Interest Level: Ages 8-12, 11-13, 9-12, 10 and up, Grades 5-9

Reading Level: 5.2, 6

Tests: Accelerated Reader, Reading Counts

Reviewed: *Horn Book*, *Kirkus*, *New York Times*, *Publishers Weekly*, *School Library Journal*

Lists: ALA Best Books for Young Adults, California Department of Education, Dekalb County, Horn Book Fanfare, Maine Student Book Awards

The Wing

Author and Illustrator: Ray Buckley

Publication: Nashville, TN: Abingdon Press, 2002

LC#: none

Editions: 0687097045 hc.

Description: Picture book, 32 pages, illustrated, 24 cm

Summary: The people of the forest are amazed at the beauty and swiftness of She Who Flies Swiftly, but one day they find her lying on the forest floor with a broken wing.

Subjects:

Healing—Fiction

Indians of North America—Fiction

Religion—Fiction

Interest Level: Ages 4-8

Chapter 2

Folklore

Folklore is an important element of traditional American Indian life. It is important to note that many traditional stories have been handed down from generation to generation. Such folk tales and legends are a part of the wisdom of the elders and usually teach a lesson rather than simply entertain.

These elders and folklore experts knew that their lessons were for all ages, not just for children. Until fairly recently, American Indian folklore was presented orally rather than in print. Most early print versions of folk tales and legends were recorded by non-Native writers, teachers, and anthropologists.

This chapter contains a number of folklore-based books by Native Americans. Readers should be aware that in some cases the Native authors have written books that deal with folklore of cultures other than their own.

Some other Native American authors and editors of folklore collections are: Catherine Attla, Percy Bullchild, Robert J. Conley, Ann M. Dunn, Charles A. Eastman, Antonio Garcez, Hitakonanu'laxk, Basil Johnson, Betty Mae Jumper, Joseph Marshall III, Marie McLaughlin, Mourning Dove, Alfonso Ortiz, Simon Otto, Alex Ramirez, Gerald Rancourt Tsonakwa, Velma Wallis, and Linda Yamane.

Baby Rattlesnake
Viborita de cascabel

Authors: Te Ata and Lynn Moroney

Illustrator: Veg Reisberg

Publication: San Francisco, CA: Children's Book Press, 1989

LC#s: 89009892 (English), 96014832 (Spanish)

Editions: 0892390492 lib. bdg., 0892391111 pb., 078571409X lib. bdg. Econo-Clad, 0892391405 pb. (Spanish), 089239143X pb. (Spanish), 0613104854 lib. bdg. Econo-Clad

Description: Picture book, 30 pages, color illustrations, 21 × 24 cm

Summary: Willful Baby Rattlesnake throws tantrums to get his rattle before he's ready, but he misuses it and learns a lesson.

Subjects:

Chickasaw Indians—Folklore

Indians of North America—Southern States—Folklore

Rattlesnakes—Folklore

Interest Level: Ages 4-8, Grades 2-5

Reading Level: 3.0

Tests: English version: Accelerated Reader, Reading Counts; Spanish version: Accelerated Reader

Reviewed: *Bloomsbury Review*, *Horn Book*, *Publishers Weekly*, *The Reading Teacher*, *San Francisco Chronicle*, *School Library Journal*

Lists: Children's Catalog (H. W. Wilson), Elementary School Library Collection

Note: Adapted by Lynn Moroney

Note: <www.cbookpress.org/ob/rattler.html>

Between Earth & Sky: Legends of Native American Sacred Places

Author: Joseph Bruchac

Illustrator: Thomas Locker

Publication: San Diego, CA: Harcourt Brace & Co., 1996

LC#: 95010862

Editions: 0152000429 lib. bdg., 0152020624 pb., 0613157311 lib. bdg. Econo-Clad

Description: Picture book, 32 pages, color illustrations, 23 × 29 cm, bibliography, author's statement, glossary, map

Summary: Through the guidance of his uncle and the retelling of various Native American legends, a young boy learns that everything living and inanimate has its place, should be considered sacred, and given respect.

Subjects:

Folklore—North America

Folklore—North America—Juvenile literature

Indians of North America—Folklore

Interest Level: Ages 4-8, Grades K-3, 2-5

Reading Level: 2.0

Tests: Accelerated Reader, Reading Counts

Reviewed: *Booklist*, *Horn Book*, *Kirkus*, *Publishers Weekly*, *School Library Journal*

Lists: NCSS-CBC Notable Children's Trade Book in Social Studies

Note: Tribes included are Wampanoag, Seneca, Navajo, Cherokee, Papago, Hopewell, Cheyenne, Hopi, Walapai, and Abenaki.

Bones in the Basket: Native Stories of the Origin of People

Author and Illustrator: C. J. Taylor

Publication: Plattsburgh, NY: Tundra Books, 1994

LC#: 94061786

Editions: 0887763278 hc., 0887764509 pb.

Description: Picture book, 32 pages, color illustrations, 29 cm

Summary: Creation stories from the Chuckchee, Cree, Mandan, Modoc, Mohawk, Osage, and Zuñi tribes.

Subjects:

Creation—Folklore

Indians of North America—Folklore

Legends—North America

Interest Level: Grades 3-7

Reading Level: 5.0

Tests: Accelerated Reader

Reviewed: *Horn Book, Kirkus, School Library Journal*

Note: French version: *Des os Dans un Panier: Légendes Amérindiennes Sur les Origines du Monde*, 0887763448

Note: Includes an information page on the seven tribes.

Brave Wolf and the Thunderbird

Author: Joe Medicine Crow

Illustrator: Linda R. Martin

Publication: Washington, D.C.: National Museum of the American Indian; New York: Abbeville Press, 1998

Series: *Tales of the People*

LC#: 98005294

Editions: 0789201607 hc.

Description: Picture book, 31 pages, illustrated, 25 cm, color maps

Summary: While hunting, Brave Wolf is snatched by a huge Thunderbird and taken to her nest on a high cliff so he can protect her chicks from a monster.

Subjects:

Crow Indians—Folklore

Folklore—Montana

Indians of North America—Montana—Folklore

Tales—Montana

Thunderbird (Legendary character)—Legends

Interest Level: Ages 4-8, Grades 2-5

Reading Level: 3.6

Tests: Accelerated Reader, Reading Counts

Reviewed: *Booklist, Horn Book, School Library Journal*

Coyote Columbus

Author: Thomas King

Illustrator: William Kent Monkman

Publication: Toronto: Douglas & McIntyre, 1992; Toronto: Groundwood Books, 2002

LC#: 2002110358

Editions: 088899155X hc.

Description: Picture book, 32 pages, illustrated

Summary: A reinterpretation of the Columbus conquest mythology as a trickster tale from the Native American point of view.

Subjects:

America—Discoveries and exploration—Spanish—Juvenile/Fiction

Columbus, Christopher—Journeys—Juvenile/Fiction

Discoveries in geography—Folklore

Explorers—America—Juvenile/Fiction

Indians of North America—History—Fiction

Interest Level: Ages 4-8, Grades 2-3

Reviewed: *Quill and Quire, Toronto Star*

Coyote in Love with a Star

Author: Martha Kreipe de Montaño
Illustrator: Tom Coffin
Publication: Washington, D.C.: National Museum of the American Indian, New York: Abbeville Press, 1998
Series: *Tales of the People*
LC#: 98005313
Editions: 0789201623 hc.
Description: Picture book, 31 pages, illustrated, 25 cm
Summary: An adaptation of a traditional tale about a Potawatomi Indian trickster-hero known to many people in the West as Coyote.
Subjects:
Coyote (Legendary character)—Legends
Indians of North America—Great Lakes Region—Folklore
Potawatomi Indians—Folklore
Interest Level: Ages 4-8, Grades P-2
Reading Level: 1.0
Reviewed: *Booklist, Dallas Morning News, Horn Book, School Library Journal*

Coyote Sings to the Moon

Author: Thomas King
Illustrator: Johnny Wales
Publication: Portland, OR: WestWinds Press, 2002
LC#: 2001057909
Editions: 155868428 hc.
Description: Picture book, 40 pages, illustrated, 27 cm
Summary: Insulted because Coyote will not sing to her, Moon leaves the sky and returns only to get away from Coyote's singing.
Subjects:
Animals—Fiction
Coyote—Fiction
Moon—Fiction
Interest Level: Ages 4-8
Lists: Oyate

Devilfish Bay: The Giant Devilfish Story: An Alaska Indian Adventure

Author: Rudy James, ThlauGooYailthThlee
Illustrators: Diana James, Rudy James, George Suckinaw James, Jr., and Embert F. James
Publication: Woodinville, WA: Wolfhouse Publishing, 1997
LC#: 97090844
Editions: 1891081004 pb.
Description: 176 pages, illustrated, 28 cm, bibliography
Summary: Two brothers exact revenge from a giant octopus in this Tlingit legend based on fact.
Subjects:
Legends—Alaska
Tlingit Indians—Folklore
Note: Author's end notes explain the background of the story. Addendum includes immigrant impact, giants of the sea reported sightings, octopus facts, sharing of the culture and traditions, and opportunities for travel in Thlee-nay-dee and Kuiu country.

Fire Race: A Karuk Coyote Tale about How Fire Came to the People

Authors: Jonathan London and Lanny Pinola
Illustrator: Sylvia Long
Publication: San Francisco, CA: Chronicle Books, 1993

LC#: 92032352

Editions: 0811802418 hc., 0613100921 lib. bdg. Econo-Clad

Description: 34 pages, color illustrations, 23 × 26 cm, bibliography

Summary: With the help of other animals, Wise Old Coyote manages to acquire fire from the wicked Yellow Jacket sisters.

Subjects:

Coyote—Legendary character—Legends

Fire—Folklore

Indians of North America—California—Folklore

Karok Indians—Folklore

Interest Level: Ages 4-8, Grades K-3

Reading Level: 4.0

Tests: Accelerated Reader

Reviewed: *Booklist*, *Horn Book*, *Kirkus*, *Publishers Weekly*, *School Library Journal*

Note: Bookbuilder's West Award, Society of Illustrators Award

Note: Afterword was written by Julian Lang.

The First Strawberries: A Cherokee Story

Author: Joseph Bruchac

Illustrator: Anna Vojtech

Publication: New York: Dial Books for Young Readers, 1993

LC#: 91031058

Editions: 0803713312 hc., 0803713320 lib. bdg., 0140564098 pb. Puffin, 0613077830 lib. bdg. Econo-Clad

Description: Picture book, 29 pages, color illustrations, 30 cm

Summary: A quarrel between the first man and the first woman is reconciled when the Sun causes strawberries to grow out of the earth.

Subjects:

Cherokee Indians—Folklore

Indians of North America—Folklore

Strawberries—Folklore

Interest Level: Ages 4-8, Grades K-3

Reading Level: 3.5

Tests: Accelerated Reader, Reading Counts

Reviewed: *Book Report*, *Booklist*, *Horn Book*, *Kirkus*, *Library Talk*, *Publishers Weekly*, *School Library Journal*

Lists: Oyate

The Flute Player: An Apache Folktale

Author and Illustrator: Michael Lacapa

Publication: Flagstaff, AZ: Rising Moon, 1990

LC#: 89063749

Editions: 0873585003 hc., 0873586271 pb., 0613035860 lib. bdg. Econo-Clad

Description: Picture book, 48 pages, color illustrations, 23 × 28 cm

Summary: Retelling of an Apache folktale of tragic love.

Subjects:

Apache Indians—Folklore

Interest Level: Ages 4-8, 9-12

Reviewed: *Horn Book*

Lists: Oyate

Flying with the Eagle, Racing the Great Bear: Stories from Native North America

Author: Joseph Bruchac

Publication: Mahwah, NJ: BridgeWater Books, 1993

LC#: 93021965

Editions: 0816730261 hc., 081673027X pb. Troll, 0785756914 lib. bdg. Econo-Clad

Description: 130 pages, illustrated, 24 cm, 16 stories

Summary: A collection of traditional tales that present the heritage of various American Indian nations, including the Wampanoag, Cherokee, Osage, Lakota, and Tlingit.

Subjects:
Indians of North America—Folklore
Indians of North America—Rites and ceremonies—Juvenile literature

Interest Level: Ages 9-12, Grades 3-7, 5-8

Reading Level: 5.3

Tests: Accelerated Reader, Reading Counts

Reviewed: *Booklist*, *The Book Report*, *Library Talk*, *Publishers Weekly*, *School Library Journal*

Lists: Oyate

Note: Tribes include Abenaki, Anishinabe, Apache, Caddo, Cherokee, Cheyenne, Dine (Navajo) Inupiaq, Iroquois, Lakota, Muskogee (Creek), Osage, Pueblo, Tlingit, Wampanoag, and Yuki.

Note: Skipping Stones Honor Award

The Ghost and Lone Warrior: An Arapaho Legend

Author and Illustrator: C. J. Taylor

Publication: Plattsburgh, NY: Tundra Books, 1991

LC#: 91065368

Editions: 0887762638 hc., 0887763081 pb., 0516081675 lib. bdg. Econo-Clad

Description: Picture book, 24 pages, color illustrations, 22 cm

Summary: Based on the legend *The Lame Warrior and the Skeleton* from *Tipi Tales of the American Indian* by D. Brown.

Subjects:
Arapaho Indians—Folklore
Indians of North America—Folklore

Interest Level: Ages 9-12, Grades 2 and up, 3-6

Reviewed: *School Library Journal*

Note: French version: *Guerrier Solitaire et le Fantame*, 088776309X pb.

Note: Includes an information page on the Arapaho.

The Girl Who Married the Moon: Tales from Native North America

Author: Joseph Bruchac and Gayle Ross

Illustrator: S. S. Burrus

Publication: Mahwah, NJ: BridgeWater Books, 1994

LC#: 93043824

Editions: 0816734801 hc., 081673481X pb. Troll, 0785778594 lib. bdg. Econo-Clad

Description: 127 pages, illustrated 24 cm, bibliography

Subjects:
Folklore—North America
Indian women—North America—Folklore
Indians of North America—Folklore

Interest Level: Ages young adult, Grades 6-8

Reviewed: *Booklist*, *Horn Book*

Grandfather's Story of Navajo Monsters

Author: Richard Red Hawk

Illustrator: Ross Coates

Publication: Sacramento: Sierra Oaks Publishing, 1988

LC#: 88061374

Editions: 0940113112 pb.

Description: Picture book, 40 pages, illustrated, 21 × 22 cm

Summary: After grandfather and his grandchildren ride horses into a canyon, look at Anasazi ruins, build a camp fire, and enjoy a meal, grandfather tells a story about Monster Slayer and Dinetah and Navajoland.

Subjects:

Folklore—Southwest, New—Juvenile literature

Monsters—Juvenile literature

Navajo Indians—Folklore—Juvenile literature

Navajo mythology—Juvenile literature

Interest Level: Ages 4-8

Grandmother Spider Brings the Sun: A Cherokee Story

Author: Geri Keams

Illustrator: James Bernardin

Publication: Flagstaff, AZ: Rising Moon, 1997

LC#: 95002978

Editions: 0873585976 hc., 0873586948 pb.

Description: Picture book, 32 pages, illustrated, 29 cm

Summary: After Possum and Buzzard fail in their attempts to steal a piece of the sun, Grandmother Spider succeeds in bringing light to the animals on her side of the world.

Subjects:

Cherokee Indians—Folklore

Folklore—United States

Indians of North America—Folklore

Sun—Folklore

Tales—Southern States

Interest Level: Ages 4-8, Grades 1-2

Reviewed: *Horn Book, Southwest Children's Review*

The Great Ball Game: A Muskogee Story

Author: Joseph Bruchac

Illustrator: Susan L. Roth

Publication: New York: Dial Books for Young Readers, 1994

LC#: 93006269

Editions: 0803715390 hc., 0803715404 lib. bdg.

Description: Picture book, 32 pages, color illustrations, 26 cm

Summary: Bat, who has both wings and teeth, plays an important part in a game between the Birds and the Animals to decide which group is better.

Subjects:

Animals—Folklore

Creek Indians—Folklore

Indians of North America—Folklore

Interest Level: Grades 3-7

Reading Level: 5.0

Tests: Accelerated Reader, Reading Counts

Reviewed: *Booklist, Horn Book, Kirkus*

The Great Spirit Horse

Author: Linda Little Wolf

Publication: Plainwell, MI: Syncopated Press, 2000

LC#: 00101725

Editions: 0967197872 pb.

Description: 156 pages, illustrated, 22 cm, glossary, 11 chapters

Subjects:

Horses—Fiction

Horses—Folklore

Indians of North America—Folklore

Interest Level: Ages 9-12

Note: Posters and activity book are also available for purchase.

Hawai'i Sings

Author: Joy S. Au
Illustrator: Doug Po'oloa Tolentino
Publication: Honolulu: Mutual Publishing, 1995
LC#: none
Editions: 1566470838 hc.
Description: Picture book, 24 pages, color illustrations, 31 cm, glossary
Summary: A creation story of how music, singing, and dance came to be.
Subjects:
American poetry
Children's poetry, American
Hawaii—Folklore
Music—Folklore
Interest Level: Ages 9-12

How Chipmunk Got His Stripes: A Tale of Bragging and Teasing

Authors: Joseph Bruchac and James Bruchac
Illustrators: Jose Aruego and Ariane Dewey
Publication: New York: Dial Books for Young Readers, 2001
LC#: 99016793
Editions: 0803724047 hc.
Description: Picture book, 32 pages, color illustrations, 21 × 26 cm
Summary: When Bear and Brown Squirrel have a disagreement about whether Bear can stop the sun from rising, Brown Squirrel ends up with claw marks on his back and becomes Chipmunk, the striped one.
Subjects:
Chipmunks—Folklore
Folklore—North America
Indians of North America—Folklore
Tales—East (U.S.)
Interest Level: Ages 4-8, 5-8, Grades K-3, 1-3
Reading Level: 2.9
Tests: Accelerated Reader, Reading Counts
Reviewed: *Booklist*, *Publishers Weekly*, *School Library Journal*
Lists: Oyate

How Raven Stole the Sun

Author: Maria Williams
Illustrator: Felix Vigil
Publication: New York: Abbeville Press, 2001
LC#: 00066348
Editions: 0789201631 hc.
Description: Picture book, 32 pages, color illustrations, 24 cm
Subjects:
Folklore—Alaska
Indians of North America—Alaska—Folklore
Tales—Alaska
Tlingit Indians—Folklore
Interest Level: Ages 4-8

How Turtle's Back Was Cracked: A Traditional Cherokee Tale

Author: Gayle Ross
Illustrator: Murv Jacob

Publication: New York: Dial Books for Young Readers, 1995

LC#: 93040657

Editions: 0803717288 hc., 0803717296 lib. bdg.

Description: Picture book, 32 pages, color illustrations, 28 cm

Summary: Turtle's shell is cracked when the wolves plot to stop his boastful ways.

Subjects:

Cherokee Indians—Folklore

Indians of North America—Folklore

Tales—Southern States

Turtles—Folklore

Interest Level: Ages 4-8, 5-8, Grades K-3

Reading Level: 4.2

Tests: Accelerated Reader, Reading Counts

Reviewed: *Booklist, Horn Book, Kirkus, Publishers Weekly, School Library Journal*

Lists: Oyate

How Two-Feather Was Saved from Loneliness: An Abenaki Legend

Author and Illustrator: C. J. Taylor

Publication: Montreal, Quebec and Plattsburgh, NY: Tundra Books, 1990

LC#: 90070138

Editions: 0887762549 hc., 0887762824 pb., 0785716157 lib. bdg. Econo-Clad

Description: Picture book, 22 pages, color illustrations, 23 cm

Summary: Retells a traditional Abenaki tale in which Two-Feather, after wandering alone all winter, meets a strange and beautiful maiden who gives him two special gifts.

Subjects:

Abenaki Indians—Folklore

Abenaki Indians—Legends

Corn—Folklore

Fire—Folklore

Indians of North America—Folklore

Interest Level: Ages 9-12

Note: French version: *Deux Plumes et la Solitude Disparue* 0887762557 hc., 0887763146 pb.

Note: Includes an information page on the Abenaki.

How We Saw the World: Nine Native Stories of the Way Things Began

Author and Illustrator: C. J. Taylor

Publication: Montreal, Quebec and Plattsburgh, NY: Tundra Books, 1993.

LC#: 92083960

Editions: 0887763022 hc., 0887763731 pb.

Description: Picture book, 32 pages, color illustrations, 29 cm

Summary: Nine legends that provide insight into how North America was seen by its first inhabitants.

Subjects:

Indian mythology—United States

Indians of North America—Folklore

Legends—United States

Interest Level: Ages 4-6, 9-12, Grades 3-7

Reading Level: 4.5

Tests: Accelerated Reader

Reviewed: *Booklist, Horn Book, Publishers Weekly, School Library Journal*

Note: French version: *Et le Cheval Nous a Ete Donne* 088776357X

Note: Includes an information page on the Algonquins, Tohono O'Odhan, Bella Coola, Micmac, Blackfoot, Oneida, Kiowa, Mohawk, and Cheyenne tribes.

Little Water and the Gift of the Animals: A Seneca Legend

Author and Illustrator: C. J. Taylor

Publication: Plattsburgh, NY: Tundra Books, 1992

LC#: 96062007

Editions: 0887764002 pb., 0613035321 lib. bdg. Econo-Clad

Description: Picture book, 24 pages, color illustrations, 22 cm

Summary: With the help of the animals, a Seneca hunter named Little Water helps his people recover from illness.

Subjects:
Seneca Indians—Legends—Juvenile literature

Interest Level: Ages 9-12, Grades 3-7

Reading Level: 3.8

Tests: Accelerated Reader

Reviewed: *Bulletin of the Center for Children's Books*, *Choice*, *Kirkus*

Note: French version: *Petit Ruisseau et le Don des Animaux*, 0887764061

The Magic Hummingbird: A Hopi Folktale

Translator: Ekkehart Malotki

Narrator: Michael Lomatuway'ma

Illustrator: Michael Lacapa

Publication: Santa Fe, NM: Kiva Publications, 1996

LC#: 95080961

Editions: 1885772041

Description: Picture book, 40 pages, color illustrations, 24 × 27 cm

Summary: Two Hopi children and a magic hummingbird bring the people back to Oraibi.

Subjects:
Folklore—Arizona
Hopi Indians—Folklore
Hummingbirds—Folklore
Indians of North America—Arizona—Folklore
Tales—Arizona—Oraibi

Interest Level: Ages 4-8, Grades 2-4

Reviewed: *School Library Journal*

Maui, the Mischief Maker

Author and Illustrator: Dietrich Varez

Publication: Honolulu, HI: Bishop Museum Press, 1991

LC#: 91072830

Editions: 0930897536 hc.

Description: 84 pages, illustrated, 28 cm

Summary: The myth of the demigod Maui, based on the Kumulipo, the ancient Hawaiian creation chant.

Subjects:
Maui (Polynesian deity)—Juvenile literature
Mythology, Hawaiian—Juvenile literature

The Messenger of Spring

Author and Illustrator: C. J. Taylor

Publication: Toronto and Plattsburgh, NY: Tundra Books, 1997

LC#: 97060508

Editions: 0887764134 hc.

Description: Picture book, 24 pages, color illustrations, 23 cm

Subjects:
Ojibwa Indians—Folklore
Tales—North America

Interest Level: Ages 9-12, Grades K-3

Reading Level: 3.3

Tests: Accelerated Reader

Note: Includes an information page on the Chippewa/Ojibwa.

The Monster from the Swamp: Native Legends of Monsters, Demons and Other Creatures

Author and Illustrator: C. J. Taylor

Publication: Plattsburgh, NY: Tundra Books, 1995

LC#: 95060980

Editions: 0884463618 hc.

Description: Picture book, 32 pages, color illustrations, 30 cm

Summary: Legends from the Cheyenne, Comanche, Gwich'in, Malecite, Micmac, Mohawk, Seneca, and Tlingit tribes.

Subjects:

Indians of North America—Legends

Legends—North America

Interest Level: Ages 9-12, Grades 3-7

Reading Level: 4.0

Tests: Accelerated Reader

Reviewed: *Horn Book*, *Multicultural Review*

Native American Animal Stories

Author: Joseph Bruchac

Illustrator: John Kahionhes Fadden

Publication: Golden, CO: Fulcrum Publishing, 1992

LC#: 92053040

Editions: 1555911277 pb.

Description: 160 pages, illustrated, 26 cm, bibliography

Subjects:

Animals—Folklore

Indians of North America—Folklore

Native American Stories

Author: Joseph Bruchac

Illustrator: John Kahionhes Fadden

Publication: Golden, CO: Fulcrum Publishing, 1991

LC#: 90085267

Editions: 1555910947 pb.

Description: 145 pages, illustrated, 26 cm, map

Summary: A collection of Native American tales and myths focusing on the relationship between man and nature.

Subjects:

Indian mythology—North America

Indians of North America—Folklore

Interest Level: Young adult

Native Plant Stories

Author: Joseph Bruchac

Illustrators: John Kahionhes Fadden and David Kanietakeron Fadden

Publication: Golden, CO: Fulcrum Publishing, 1995

LC#: 94023483

Editions: 1555912125 pb.

Description: 160 pages, illustrated, 26 cm, map

Subjects:

Indians of North America—Folklore

Plants—Folklore

Tales—North America

Interest Level: Grades 4-8, young adult

Reviewed: *Booklist*

Old Father Story Teller

Author and Illustrator: Pablita Velarde
Publication: Santa Fe, NM: Clear Light Publishers, 1989
LC#s: 89086056, 92021175
Editions: 0940666103 hc., 0940666243 pb.
Description: 56 pages, color illustrations, 23 × 30 cm
Summary: Includes retelling of six Tewa Indian legends and a brief biographical section about the author, who is a noted Native American artist.
Subjects:
Folklore—New Mexico—Santa Clara Pueblo
Indians of North America, Southwest, New—Folklore
Tewa Indians—Folklore
Interest Level: Ages 4-8, 9-12

One More Story: Contemporary Seneca Tales of the Supernatural

Author: DuWayne Leslie Bowen
Illustrator: Beth Clark
Publication: Greenfield Center, NY: Greenfield Review Press
LC#: 89089021
Editions: 091267878X pb.
Description: 50 pages, illustrated, 23 cm
Subjects:
Folklore—New York State
Ghost stories, American—New York State
Indians of North America—New York State—Folklore
Seneca Indians—Folklore
Tales—New York State
Lists: Oyate

Rabbit's Wish for Snow: A Native American Legend

Author: Tchin
Illustrator: Carolyn Ewing
Publication: New York: Scholastic, 1996
Series: *Hello Reader*, Level 3
LC#: 96024746
Editions: 0590697676 pb., 0613086090 lib. bdg. Econo-Clad
Description: Picture book, 32 pages, illustrated, 23 cm
Summary: Retells the Native American folktale that explains how rabbits came to look as they do today.
Subjects:
Folklore—North America
Indians of North America—Folklore
Rabbits—Folklore
Interest Level: Ages 4-8, Grades K-2, P-2
Reading Level: 1.8
Tests: Reading Counts

The Secret of the White Buffalo: An Oglala Legend

Author: C. J. Taylor
Publication: Plattsburgh, NY: Tundra Books, 1997
LC#: 96062009
Editions: 0887763995 pb., 0887763219 hc., 061303533X lib. bdg. Econo-Clad
Description: Picture book, 24 pages, illustrated, 23 cm
Subjects:
Oglala Sioux Indians
Interest Level: Ages 5-8, Ages 9-12
Reviewed: *Booklist*, *Horn Book*
Note: French versions: *Le Secret du Bison Blanc* 0887764053 pb., 0887763227 hc (Canada), 2904292918 hc (France)

Note: Includes an information page on the Oglala Sioux.

Spirit of the Cedar People: More Stories and Paintings of Chief Lelooska

Author: Chief Lelooska and Christine Normandin, editor
Publication: New York: DK Publications, 1998
LC#: 98003522
Editions: 0789425718 hc.
Description: 38 pages, color illustrations, 33 cm, 1 audio CD disc
Summary: none
Subjects:
Indians of North America—Northwest Coast of North America—Folklore
Tales—Northwest Coast of North America
Interest Level: Ages 9-12
Reviewed: *Horn Book*

The Story of the Milky Way: A Cherokee Tale

Authors: Joseph Bruchac and Gayle Ross
Illustrator: Virginia A. Stroud
Publication: New York: Dial Books for Young Readers, 1995
LC#: 94020926
Editions: 0803717377 hc., 0803717385 lib. bdg.
Description: Picture book, 32 pages, color illustrations, 28 cm
Summary: When cornmeal is stolen from an elderly couple, the others in a Cherokee village find a way to drive off the thief, creating the Milky Way in the process.

Subjects:
Cherokee Indians—Folklore
Folklore—United States
Indians of North America—Folklore
Milky Way—Folklore
Interest Level: Ages 4-8, Grades K-3
Reading Level: 3.8
Tests: Accelerated Reader
Reviewed: *Booklist*, *Horn Book*, *Kirkus*

The Turkey Girl: A Zuni Cinderella Story

Author: Penny Pollock
Illustrator: Ed Young
Publication: Boston: Little, Brown, 1996
LC#: 93028947
Editions: 0316713147 hc.
Description: Picture book, 32 pages, color illustrations, 29 cm
Summary: In this American Indian variant of a familiar story, some turkeys make a gown of feathers for the poor girl who tends them so that she can participate in a sacred dance, but they desert her when she fails to return as promised.
Subjects:
Cinderella (Tale)
Indians of North America—New Mexico—Folklore
Zuni Indians—Folklore
Interest Level: Ages 4-8, 6-8, Grades K-3, 4-6
Reading Level: 2.0
Tests: Accelerated Reader, Reading Counts
Reviewed: *Booklist*, *Horn Book*, *Kirkus*

When Hopi Children Were Bad: A Monster Story

Authors: Tawa Mana and Youyouseyah
Illustrator: Ross Coates
Publication: Sacramento, CA: Sierra Oaks Publishing, 1989
LC#: 89062046
Editions: 0940113201 pb.
Description: Picture book, 41 pages, illustrated, 21 cm
Summary: A Hopi grandfather tells his grandchildren the story of the giant kachinas—an ancient Hopi tale of monsters that come to eat bad children.
Subjects:
Hopi Indians—Fiction
Hopi Indians—Folklore
Indians of North America—Fiction
Indians of North America—Folklore
Monsters—Fiction
Interest Level: Ages 9-12

When the Chenoo Howls: Native American Tales of Terror

Author: Joseph Bruchac
Illustrator: William Sauts Netam'xwe Bock
Publication: New York: Walker & Co., 1998
LC#: 97048715
Editions: 0802786383 hc., 0802775764 pb.
Description: 128 pages, illustrated, 24 cm, bibliography
Subjects:
Folklore
Folklore—Northeastern States
Indians of North America—Northeastern States—Folklore
Monsters—Folklore
Monsters—Juvenile literature
Tales—Northeastern States
Woodland Indians—Folklore
Interest Level: Grades 3-6

Chapter 3

Storytelling and Drama

This chapter includes storytelling and drama, modern extensions of the oral tradition. It is important for non-Native Americans to give both stories and tribal storytellers respect, just as religions of all cultures should be respected. Much of the literature in this chapter is folklore presented through sound and video recordings. This chapter includes books, sound recordings, and videos. Some subjects have been omitted to conserve space. Readers may assume that items herein are about "Indians of North America" and "folklore." "Performer/storyteller" has been used rather than "author." Interest levels have been added when available; reading levels are not applicable to recordings.

A pioneer was Cherokee writer Lynn Riggs, author of *Green Grow the Lilacs*, on which the musical *Oklahoma* was based. A look at the published works of drama by Native American authors shows only a few authors, and several of those are Canadian authors. The following names represent some published and unpublished Native Americans in the field of drama: Annette Arkeketa, Jason Begay, Diane Benson, Fred Bigjim, Tsianina Redstone Blackstone, Marie Clements, Bunky Echo-Hawk, Hanay Geiogamah, Diane Glancy, Terry Gomez, Anthony Higheagle, Tomson Highway, Phillip Hooser, Matthew Jones, Arthur Junaluska, John Kauffman, Victoria Kneubuhl, Theodore Kottke, Owen Le Beau, Eric Linklater, Larry Loyie, Vera Manuel, Lisa Mayo, John McLeod, Gloria Miguel, Monique Mojica, Denise Mosely, Yvette Nolan, Judy Lee Oliva, Helen Owens, Robert Owens, Sandra Peters, George Phelps, Lynda Poolaw, Liz Reese, Marcie Rendon, Armand Ruffo, Lola Shropshire, Robert Shorty, Sharon Shorty, Drew Hayden Taylor, Alice Timmons, Wallace Tucker, E. Donald Two-Rivers, Diane Way, Marion Weber, Sadie Worn Staff, Rhiana Yazzie, and William S. Yellow Robe.

Cherokee Children's Songs

Storyteller: George Vann, Tsatsi

Publication: Richardson, TX: Various Indian Peoples Publishing, 2002

LC#: none

Editions: 1884655009

Description: Audio CD and song book in English and Cherokee

Contents: The Rabbit Song, The Little Bird Song, Chickadee, The Geese Song, The Hoot Owl Song, Quail's Song, The Bear Song, The Wolf Song, The Snake Song, The Little People Song, The Rain Song, and Cherokee Lull-a-bye.

Cherokee Scary Stories

Storyteller: Gregg Howard

Publication: Richardson, TX: Various Indian Peoples Publishing, 2000

LC#: none

Editions: 1884655459

Description: Audio CD, 52 minutes

Contents: Introduction, "Ulaguhn" Origin of Yellow Jackets, Eagle's Revenge, Davie's Tale, "Dotsuwa" Daughter of the Sun, The Hunter and the "Tianuwa," the Nest of the "Tianuwa," The Hunter and the "Dakwa," "Utlunta" Spear Finger, The Snake Man, "Atagahi" The Enchanted Lake, Closing.

The Choctaw Way

Storyteller: Tim Tingle

Publication: Canyon Lake, TX: Storytribe Publishing, nd.

LC#: none

Editions: none

Description: Audio cassette

Contents: Side A: Raccoon Chant/Chief Webb's Lament, Amazing Grace, Trail of Tears, Meeting with Reptiles/Snake Chant, New Puppy; Side B: Saltypie, Amazing Grace, The Choctaw Way.

Interest Level: Ages 12 and up

Coyote and Rock and Other Lushootseed Stories

Storyteller: Vi Hilbert

Publication: New York: HarperChildren's Audio, 1992, 1996

Series: *Parabola Storytime*

LC#: none

Editions: 1559945397

Description: Audio cassette, 60 minutes

Contents: Lady Louise Cleans House, Lifting the Sky, Bear and Fishhawk, Boil and Hammer, Coyote and Rock, Owl and His Wife Frog, Mud Swallow's House, Little Raccoon, Skunk's Important Information.

Echoes of the Night: Native American Legends of the Night Sky

Storyteller: Gerald Rancourt Tsonakwa

Publication: Bellingham, WA: Soundings of the Planet, 1987, 1992

LC#: none

Editions: none

Description: Audio CD, 49 minutes

Contents: Sit By My Fire, Maheo, Creation Story, Coyote, Seven Sisters, Kuloscap & The Ghosts, My Brother The Bear, Shining Way, Silent Dreams.

Note: Algonkian (Algonquian), Hopi, Ojibway, Abenaki

The Elders Speak: Dakotah and Ojibway Stories of the Land

Performers/Storytellers: Gourd Woman, Mary Louise Defender Wilson, and Eagle Heart, Francis Cree

Publication: Bismarck, ND: Makoché Word, 1999

LC#: 2001559220

Editions: none

Description: Enhanced CD, 66 minutes

Contents: Introductory Remarks, Sky Woman and the Great Flood, The Powerful Lake, The White Buffalo, The Woman Who Turned Herself to Stone, Holy Spring, The Spiderwoman and the Giant, Nanabosho and the Dancing Ducks, Coyote's Den Hill.

Note: NAMMY Award Winner, Best Spoken Word

Fireside Tales: More Lessons from the Animal People

Storyteller: Dovie Thomason Sickles

Publication: Cambridge, MA: Yellow Moon Press, 2001

Editions: 0938756583 audio cassette; 0938756291 audio CD

Description: Audio cassette, audio CD, 67 minutes

Contents: Side 1: Fox & Goldfinch, Buffalo & Turtle, Bear & Chipmunk; Side 2: Mice Make Peace, Why There Are Bats, Frog's Teeth, Dog's Tails.

The Gift of the Great Spirit: Iroquois Lesson Stories

Storyteller: Tehanetorens, Ray Fadden

Publication: Greenfield Center, NY: Good Mind Records, 1988

LC#: none

Editions: none

Description: Audio cassette, 50 minutes

Contents: Side 1: The Story of the Monster Bear: Introduction, The Time for Telling Stories, In the Longhouse, The Story of the Monster Bear, Six Nations Singers, The Fierce Beast, In the Longhouse; Side 2: The Gift of the Great Spirit: Introduction, The Hermit Thrush, The Gift of the Great Spirit, Six Nations Singers, Record Belts, Disciplining Children.

Gluskabe Stories

Storyteller: Joseph Bruchac

Publication: Cambridge, MA: Yellow Moon Press, 1990

LC#: none

Editions: 0938756265

Description: Audio cassette

Interest Level: Ages 8 and up

Contents: Gluskabe & the Creator, Gluskabe's Game Bag, Gluskabe Changes the Animals, The Four Wishes, Gluskabe & Dzidziz, The Maple Syrup, Gluskabe & the Skunk, The Water Monster, Gluskabe & Tobacco, The Wind Eagle.

Grandfather Sings-Alone's Favorite Tales

Storyteller: Duncan Sings-Alone

Publication: Hopkinton, MA: Two Canoes Press, 1999

LC#: none

Editions: 1929590024 audio CD; 192950032 audio cassette

Description: Audio CD or audio cassette

Note: Parents' Choice Award, NAMMY Award nominee

Grandfather's Stories

Storyteller: Gregg Howard

Publication: Richardson, TX: Various Indian Peoples Publishing, 1998

LC#: none

Editions: 1884655289

Description: Audio CD

Contents: Intro, Origin of Fire, The Ballgame of Animals & Birds, Why Mole Lives Underground, Why Rabbit Has a Short Tail, Why Possum's Tail Is Bare, Little Turtle, How Deer Got His Antlers, Why Bat Flies at Night.

Grandma Spider Brings the Fire

Storyteller: Tim Tingle

Publication: Canyon Lake, TX: Storytribe Publishing, nd.

LC#: none

Editions: none

Description: Audio cassette

Contents: Side A: White Wolf, Coyote Meets the Rock, Mud Pony Boy; Side B: Rabbit and Buffalo, First Robin, Grandma Spider Brings the Fire.

Interest Level: Ages 5-12

How Rabbit Tricked Otter and Other Cherokee Animal Stories

Storyteller: Gayle Ross

Publication: New York: HarperChildren's Audio, 1991, 1996

Series: *Parabola Storytime*

LC#: 93717863

Editions: 1559945427

Description: Audio cassette, 60 minutes

Contents: Flint Visits Rabbit, How Rabbit Tricked Otter, How Deer Won His Antlers, Why Deer's Teeth Are Blunt, Why Possum's Tail Is Bare, The Origin of the Bear, The Hunter and the Bear, Bear Dines with Rabbit, How Turtle's Back Was Cracked.

Inktomi and the Ducks and Other Assiniboin Trickster Stories

Storyteller: Ron Evans

Publication: New York: Society for the Study of Myth and Tradition, 1994

Series: *Parabola Storytime*

LC#: 99590755

Editions: 0930407334

Description: Audio cassette, 60 minutes

Contents: Inktomi Eats Shadowfish Soup, Inktomi the Grass-Dancer, Inktomi and the Ducks, Inktomi Tries Beaver's Fur Coat Magic, Inktomi Finds New Eyeballs, Inktomi Helps Mouse.

Iroquois Stories

Storyteller: Joseph Bruchac

Publication: Greenfield Center, NY: Good Mind Records, 1988

LC#: none

Editions: none

Description: Audio cassette, 46 minutes

Contents: Side One: Tales from the Longhouse: Introduction, The Creation, How Buzzard Got His Feathers, Turtle's Race with Bear, Raccoon and the Crayfish; Side Two: Iroquois Women's Stories: The Wife of the Thunderer, The Brave Woman and the Flying Head.

Lessons from the Animal People

Storyteller: Dovie Thomason

Publication: Cambridge, MA: Yellow Moon Press, Corn Beans & Squash Music, 1996

LC#: 99595520

Editions: 0938756508 cassette; 0938756516 CD

Description: Audio cassette, audio CD

Contents: The Making of the Animals, Ant Dances for Light, The Beaver Woman & the Eagle, Mouse & the Moon, The War Party, Turtle Learns to Fly, Two Chipmunks, The Bear Child, Frog & Turtle.

Reviewed: Audiofile

Note: ALA Notable Children's Recording, Audiofile Editor's Choice Award

Note: Available as an audio download.

Medicine Path: Healing Songs and Stories of the Northwest Native Americans

Storyteller: Johnny Moses

Publication: Boulder, CO: Sounds True, 1997

LC#: none

Editions: 154555038

Description: Audio cassette, 59 minutes

Contents: Indian Shaker Song for Soul Loss; Healing Song from the Caves; The Grandmother Story; Seeking a Guardian Spirit; Learning from Plants, Animals, and the Elements; A Wolf Song; Healing of the Heart Song; Songs as Cries to the Creator and Mother Earth; More.

My Relatives Say: Traditional Dakotah Stories

Storyteller: Mary Louise Defender Wilson

Publication: Bismarck, ND: Makoché Word, 2001

LC#: none

Editions: 0965087271

Description: Enhanced CD, 59 minutes

Contents: The World Never Ends, The Blue Heron Who Stayed for the Winter, Earth Beans, The Dakotah Have Had Horses for a Long Time, How Snake Creek Came to Be, Why the Fawn Has Spots, The Star in the Cottonwood Tree, The First Flute Was Used for Courting.

Octopus Lady and Crow: And Other Animal People Stories of the Northwest Coast

Storyteller: Johnny Moses
Publication: New York: Society for the Study of Myth and Tradition, 1994
Series: *Parabola Storytime*
LC#: 95705841
Editions: 0930407342
Description: Audio cassette, 60 minutes
Contents: Octopus Lady and Crow, Bear Man and Ant Lady, The Swan Story, The Berry People, The People Story, The Basket Ogress, The Ticklish Bear, Bear and Crow, The Dreamtime Story.
Interest Level: Ages 8 and up
Reviewed: *Audiofile*

Pushing Up the Sky: Seven Native American Plays for Children

Author: Joseph Bruchac
Illustrator: Teresa Flavin
Publication: New York: Dial Books for Young Readers, 2000
LC#: 98020483
Editions: 0803721684 lib. bdg., 0803725353 pb.
Description: 96 pages, illustrated, 26 cm, bibliography
Summary: Uses drama to tell seven different stories from Native American traditions including the Abenaki, Ojibway, Cherokee, Cheyenne, Snohomlish, Tlingit, and Zuni.
Subjects: Children's plays, American Indians of North America—Juvenile/Drama Plays
Interest Level: Ages 9-12
Reviewed: *Booklist*

Sacred Twins and Spider Woman: and Other Navajo Creation Stories

Storyteller: Geri Keams
Publication: New York: HarperChildren's Audio, 1992, 1996
Series: *Parabola Storytime*
LC#: none
Editions: 1559946784
Description: Audio cassette, 60 minutes
Contents: Side One: Creation of First Man, First Woman; Hunter Boy Meets Rabbit Man; Sacred Twins and Spider Woman; Side Two: Coyote Brings Fire, Snail Carries Water.

The Story of the Inchworm: A Traditional Cherokee Indian Story

Storytellers: Driver Pheasant and Daniel Pheasant
Publication: Richardson, TX: Various Indian Peoples Publishing, 1999
Series: *Across the Fire*
LC#: none
Editions: 1884655564
Description: Audio CD and booklet in English and Cherokee

Tales of Wonder: Traditional Native American Stories for Children

Storyteller: Gregg Howard
Publication: Dallas, TX: Rich-Heape Films, 1998
Series: *Circle of Life*
LC#: none
Editions: none
Description: Video tape, 60 minutes; audio CD, 60 minutes
Contents: Rabbit & Bear, Rabbit's Short Tail, Why Possum's Tail Is Bare, The Ruby Necklace, Origin of Fire, Pleiades and the Pine Tree, Little Gray Bat, Little Turtle, How Deer Got Antlers.
Reviewed: *Native Peoples Magazine, School Library Journal, Video Librarian*
Note: Video: *Parenting Magazine* Video of the Year 2000, National Parenting Publications Award 1999, Parent's Guide to Children's Media Award

Tales of Wonder II: Traditional Native American Stories for Children

Storyteller: Gregg Howard
Publication: Dallas, TX: Riche-Heap Films, 2000
Series: *Circle of Life*
LC#: none
Editions: none
Description: Video tape, 60 minutes
Contents: Dream Catcher, Daughter of the Sun, Democracy, Sky People, Strawberries, Hawk and the Hunter.

Tell Me a Tale: A Book about Storytelling

Author: Joseph Bruchac
Publication: San Diego: Harcourt Brace, 1997
LC#: 96021697
Editions: 0152012214 hc.
Description: 119 pages, 22 cm, bibliography
Summary: Storyteller Joseph Bruchac incorporates many of his favorite tales in this discussion of the four basic components of storytelling: listening, observing, remembering, and sharing.
Subjects:
Folklore
Storytelling
Tales
Reviewed: *Booklist, Horn Book*

Who Speaks for Wolf: A Native American Learning Story

Author: Paula Underwood
Illustrator: Frank Howell
Publication: Austin, TX: Tribe of Two Press, 1983; San Anselmo, CA: Tribe of Two Press, 1991, 1994
LC#s: 83051684, 91065522, 94078236
Editions: 1879678012 pb. (2nd ed.), 187967808X pb. (story teller's ed.)
Description: 51 pages, illustrated, 24 cm
Summary: An Indian tribe learns an important lesson after it ignores a hunter's warning and settles in the heart of a great community of wolves.
Subjects:
Folklore—North America

Indians of North America—Folklore
Oneida Indians—Folklore
Interest Level: All ages

Wopila: A Giveaway Lakota Stories

Storyteller: Dovie Thomason
Publication: Cambridge, MA: Yellow Moon Press, 1993

LC#: none
Editions: 0938756443 audio cassette
Description: Audio cassette, 60 minutes
Interest Level: Ages 7 and up
Contents: Introduction, The Pet Donkey, The Spirit Wife, The Rabbit People, Iya (Camp Eater), Inktomi & Buzzard, Inktomi & Ducks & Rock, Inktomi Changes His Mind.
Note: Parents' Choice Award

American Indian Storytellers

This list includes only those storytellers who have Internet Web sites. Storytellers living in Canada or Europe have not been included. Readers seeking traditional storytellers to provide programs may find the cultural centers listed on the Web helpful. This list is not all-inclusive and should be considered merely a starting point for those interested in scheduling a storyteller.

Lloyd Arneach (Cherokee)
<www.turnerlearning.com/turnersouth/storytelling/lloyd.html>

Autumn Morning Star (Blackfeet, Choctaw)
<www.angelfire.com/celeb/magicmorningstar/AMS.HTML>

Badger Woman (Blackfoot)
<www.homestead.com/BadgerWomansWeb/Intro.html>

Tucson Big Mountain (Mohawk, Apache, Comanche)
<www.lapuppet.com/Native%20dreams.htm>

Blackhawk [Walters] (Choctaw, Creek)
<www.yamd.org/blackhawk.html>

James (Jim) Bruchac (Abenaki)
<www.ndakinna.com/storytelling.html>

Joseph Bruchac (Abenaki)

Marge (Margaret) Bruchac (Abenaki)
<www.avcnet.org/ne-do-ba/wa_02.html>

Donna Cross (Sac, Fox) and Joe Cross (Caddo, Potawatomi)
<http://members.tripod.com/leafarrow/>

Jackalene Crow Hiendlmayr (Cherokee, Creek)
<www.nativestyles.com/aboutus.htm>

Paul Eddy (Yankton Dakota)
    <www.indiotrail.org/voice.htm>

Dayton Edmonds (Caddo)
    <www.daytonedmonds.com>

Ron Evans (Chippewa, Cree, Assiniboin)
    <www.ipl.org/cgi/ref/native/browse.pl/A253>

Jack Gladstone (Blackfeet)

Bobby Gonzalez (Puerto Rican, Taino)

Harvest Moon (Quinault)
    <www.humanities.org/inquiringmind/moon.html>

Onehawk Hirajeta (Comanche)
    <www.angelfire.com/ca/4winds/page4.html>

Gregg Howard (Cherokee, Powhatan)
    <http://hometown.aol.com/vipublish/Kanohesgiaol.html>

Rudy James (Tlingit)
    <http://home.earthlink.net/~wolfhouse/author.html>

Matthew "Sitting Bear" Jones (Kiowa, Otoe, Missouria)
    <www.lincolnne.com/nonprofit/nhc/speakers.html>

Geri Keams (Navajo)
    <www.iusd.k12.ca.us/career/lessons/subjects/l-arts/Author/gerikeam.htm>

Bertney Langley (Koasati)
    <www.nsula.edu/folklife/database/biography/langleyB.html>

Kevin Locke (Lakota Anishinabe)
    <www.kevinlocke.com/locke.htm>

Jerry Thundercloud McDonald (Mohawk)
    <www.lotusarts.com/jerry.htm>

Medicine Story (Wampanoag)
    <http://ne-arts.net/nhsc/ROSTER/MED.HTM>

Ramona Moore Big Eagle (Tuscarora)
    <http://indiantrailonline.com/eagletales.htm>

Lynn Moroney (Chickasaw)
    <http://solar-center.stanford.edu/folklore/moroney.html>

Johnny Moses (Tulalip Nootka, Saanich, Snohomish, Dwamish, Chehamus)
    <www.johnnymoses.com/lowres/index.html>

Jess Walking Horse Palamino (Shoshone, Mescalero Apache) and Fred Running Bear Popejoy (many Indian nations)
    <www.bigrockcreekcamp.com/grandfth.htm>
    <www.jtmedia.com/angstrom/talent/talent.html#anchor1577252>

Red Hawk (Cherokee)
    <www.redhawkspeaks.com/edu.html>

Gayle Ross (Cherokee)
    <www.classactsarts.org/artists/gaylepg.html>

Alan Salazar (Chumash, Tataviam)
<www.nps.gov/samo/fos/salazar.html>

Fred Shaw (Shawnee)
<http://la.lti.cs.cmu.edu/callan/k12/ScavHunt2/nsnatura/shawasp.htm>

Jerry Shaw (Osage)
<criminaljustice.wichita.edu/ethnicweb/ethnicfac/js.htm>

Abel Silvas Running Grunion (Juaneño)
<www.nps.gov/samo/fos/abelbio.html>

Duncan Sings-Alone (Cherokee)
<www.twocanoespress.com/present.html>

Terry Tafoya (Taos, Warm Springs)
<www.tamanawit.com>

Tchin (Blackfoot Narragansett)
<http://hometown.aol.com/tchinart/contact.htm>

Dovie Thomason (Sickles) (Kiowa, Apache, Lakota)
<www.yaconn.org/dovie_thomason.htm>

Tim Tingle (Choctaw)
<http://talesandlegends.net/direct.html#Tingle>

Georgiana Valoyce-Sanchez (Chumash, Papago, Tohono O'odham)
<www.csulb.edu/colleges/cla/ais/bio-georgiana.html>

Ralph Williston (Choctaw)
<www.little-eagle.com/default.htm>

Chapter 4

Poetry and Anthologies

This chapter lists books of poetry written specifically for young readers by Native American writers. A list of American Indian literature anthologies, which contain both poetry and prose, follows the individual book listings.

Early-day American Indian poets are Emily Pauline Johnson (1861-1913), Alexander Lawrence Posey (1873-1908), John Rollin Ridge (1827-1867), and Rolla Lynn Riggs (1899-1954). Other American Indian poets are: Carroll Arnett, Marilou Awiakta, Carol Bachofner, Marie Annharte Baker, Charles Ballard, Jim Barnes, Diane Benson, Fred Bigjim, Duane BigEagle, Gloria Bird, Kimberly Blaeser, Peter Blue Cloud, James Blue Wolf, William Borden, Besmilr Brigham, Silvester Brito, Diane Burns, Barney Bush, Gladys Cardiff, Chrystos, Susan Clements, Allison Hedge Coke, Charlotte Declue, Anita Endrezze, Heid Erdrich, Jennifer Eyen, Nia Francisco, Della Frank, Chief Dan George, Roxy Gordon, Garry Gottfriedson, Janice Gould, Catron Grieves, Raven Hail, Gordon Henry, Inés Hernández-Avila, Nora Hunter, Alex Jacobs, Rex Jim, Rita Joe, Roberta Joe, Janet Johnson, Moses Jumper, Mike Kabotie, Maurice Kenny, Wayne Keon, Harold Littlebird, Evelina Lucero, Victoria Manyarrows, David Martinson, Janet McAdams, Wilma McDaniel, June McGlashan, Tiffany Midge, Deborah Miranda, Joe Tate, nila northSun, William Oandasan, Louis Oliver, Gus Palmer, Elise Paschen, Anna Price, Howard Rainer, Carter Revard, Wendy Rose, Ralph Salisbury, Carol Lee Sanchez, Edgar Silex, Leslie Silko, Michael Simpson, John Smelcer, Patricia Smith, R. T. Smith, Denise Sweet, Mary TallMountain, Earle Thompson, Laura Tohe, Haunani-Kay Trask, Gail Tremblay, Mark Turcotte, Roy Henry Vickers, Ron Welburn, Roberta Hill, Karenne Wood, Elizabeth Woody, Ray Young Bear, Greg Young-Ing, and Ofelia Zepeda.

Circle of Thanks

Author: Joseph Bruchac
Illustrator: Murv Jacob
Publication: Mahwah, NJ: BridgeWater Books, 1996
LC#: 95041175
Editions: 0816740127 hc.
Description: Picture book, 32 pages, color illustrations, 27 cm
Summary: Fourteen poems with themes of thanksgiving and appreciation of nature, based in part on traditional Native American songs and prayers.
Subjects:
American poetry
Children's poetry, American
Gratitude—Juvenile/Poetry
Indians of North American—Juvenile/Poetry
Nature—Juvenile/Poetry
Interest Level: Ages 4-8, Grades 1-5
Reviewed: *Booklist*, *Kirkus*

Dancing Teepees: Poems of American Indian Youth

Author: Native American youth, selected by Virginia Driving Hawk Sneve
Illustrator: Stephen Gammell
Publication: New York: Holiday House, 1989
LC#: 88011075
Editions: 0823407241 lib. bdg., 0823408795 pb.
Description: 32 pages, color illustrations, 21 × 26 cm
Summary: An illustrated collection of poems from the oral tradition of Native Americans.
Subjects:
Children's poetry, Indian—United States—Translations into English
Indian poetry—Collections
Indian poetry—Translations into English
Indians of North America—Juvenile/Poetry
Interest Level: Ages 4-8, Grades K-3
Reading Level: 3.0
Tests: Reading Counts
Reviewed: *Booklist*, *Multicultural Review*, *School Library Journal*
Lists: ALA Notable Books, *Booklist* Editor's Choice, H. W. Wilson's Children's Catalog and Elementary School Library Collection, National Council of Social Studies, *School Library Journal's* Best Books

The Earth Under Sky Bear's Feet: Native American Poems of the Land

Author: Joseph Bruchac
Illustrator: Thomas Locker
Publication: New York: Philomel Books, 1995
LC#: 94009943
Editions: 039922713X lib. bdg., 069811647X pb., 0613105036 lib. bdg. Econo-Clad
Description: 32 pages, illustrated, 29 cm, bibliography
Summary: A retelling of twelve tales from various North American Indian cultures describing how Sky Bear, the Big Dipper, sees the Earth from the sky.
Subjects:
Indian poetry—North American
Indians of North America—Folklore
Folklore—North America
Nature—Folklore

Stars—Folklore
Tales—North America
Ursa major—Folklore

Interest Level: Ages 4-8, Grades 3-5

Reviewed: *Booklist, Horn Book, Midwest Book Review*

Last Leaf First Snowflake to Fall

Author and Illustrator: Leo Yerxa

Publication: New York: Orchard Books, 1994; Toronto: Groundwood, 1993

LC#: 92005775

Editions: 0531068242 hc. (Orchard), 0531086747 lib. bdg. (Orchard), 0888991835 hc. (Groundwood)

Description: Picture book, 32 pages, color illustrations, 32 cm

Summary: An American Indian parent and child move through the forest and over a pond as nature passes from fall to winter.

Subjects:

Children's poetry, Canadian
Indians of North America—Fiction
Nature—Fiction
Seasons—Juvenile poetry
Winter—Fiction

Interest Level: Ages 4-8, 5-8, 8-11

Reviewed: *Booklist, Horn Book, Kirkus*

Note: Amelia Frances Howard-Gibbon Medal Canadian Association of Children's Librarians, Mr. Christie's Book Award Best Canadian Children's Book

Mama is Hāpai

Author: Chaika Piilani Hale

Illustrator: Dennis Asato

Publication: Honolulu: Anoai Press, 1998

LC#: none

Editions: 0965397122 hc.

Description: Picture book, A Lift-A-Flap book, 32 pages, color illustrations, 26 cm, glossary, computer generated art

Summary: In rhyming verse, a Hawaiian girl tells the story of her mother's pregnancy.

Subjects:

Babies—Juvenile poetry
Family—Juvenile poetry
Hawaii—Fiction
Mother and child—Fiction
Pregnancy—Fiction

Interest Level: Baby-preschool

Reviewed: *Honolulu Star-Bulletin, Honolulu Weekly*

Rising Voices: Writings of Young Native Americans

Editors: Arlene B. Hirschfelder and Beverly R. Singer

Publication: New York: Scribners, 1992

LC#: 91032083

Editions: 0684192071 lib. bdg., 0804111677 pb.

Description: 115 pages, 22 cm, index

Summary: A collection of poems and essays in which young Native Americans speak of their identity, their families and communities, rituals, and the harsh realities of their lives.

Subjects:

American literature—20th century
American literature—Indian authors—Collections
Children's writings
Indian youth—United States—Poetry
Indians of North America—Literary collections
Youth's writings, American

Interest Level: Ages 9-12, 12 and up

Reviewed: *Horn Book, Kirkus*

Songs of Shiprock Fair

Author: Luci Tapahonso
Illustrator: Anthony Chee Emerson
Publication: Walnut, CA: Kiva Publishing, 1999
LC#: 99063989
Editions: 1885772114 hc.
Description: Picture book, 32 pages, color illustrations, 26 cm
Summary: A young Navajo girl enjoys every part of the annual Shiprock Fair, including the dances, parade, carnival, exhibits, contests, food and the chance to visit with relatives.
Subjects:
Fairs—New Mexico—Shiprock—Juvenile poetry
Navajo Indians—New Mexico—Shiprock—Juvenile poetry
Shiprock (NM)—Juvenile/Poetry
Interest Level: Ages 4-8
Reading Level: 4.9
Tests: Accelerated Reader
Reviewed: *Horn Book*
Lists: Oyate

Thirteen Moons on Turtle's Back

Authors: Joseph Bruchac and Jonathan London
Illustrator: Thomas Locker
Publication: New York: Philomel Books, 1992
LC#: 91003991
Editions: 0399221417 lib. bdg., 0698115848 pb.
Description: 32 pages, color illustrations, 29 cm
Summary: Celebrates the seasons of the year through poems from the legends of such Native American tribes as the Cherokee, Cree, and Sioux.
Subjects:
American poetry—Collections
Children's poetry, American
Indians of North America—Folklore
Indians of North America—Folklore—Juvenile/Poetry
Indians of North America—Poetry
Seasons—Juvenile/Poetry
Interest Level: Ages 4-8, 7-9, Grades K-3
Reading Level: 4.0
Tests: Accelerated Reader, Reading Counts
Reviewed: *Horn Book*, *Kirkus*, *School Library Journal*
Lists: Choice, National Council for Social Studies Award, Reading Rainbow

When the Moon Is Full: A Lunar Year

Author: Penny Pollock
Illustrator: Mary Azarian
Publication: Boston: Little, Brown, 2001
LC#: 00028238
Editions: 0317712171 lib. bdg.
Description: 32 pages, illustrated, 26 cm
Subjects:
Months—Folklore
Moon—Folklore
Seasons—Folklore
Interest Level: Ages 4-8, 5-8, Grades K-3, K-4
Reading Level: 2.0
Reviewed: *Booklist*, *Kirkus*, *Publishers Weekly*, *School Library Journal*

When the Rain Sings: Poems by Young Native Americans

Publication: New York: Simon & Schuster Books for Young Readers, 1999

LC#: 98031784

Editions: 0689822839 lib. bdg.

Description: 96 pages, color illustrations, 21 cm, indexes

Summary: A collection of poems written by young Native Americans, inspired by or matched with photographs of artifacts and people from the National Museum of the American Indian.

Subjects:

American poetry—20th century

Children's poetry, American—Indian authors

Children's writings

Children's writings, American

Indians of North America—Antiquities—Juvenile poetry

Indians of North America—Poetry

Youths' writings, American

Interest Level: Grades 3-7

Reading Level: 4.0

Reviewed: *Horn Book*, *School Library Journal*

Lists: National Council of Social Studies

American Indian Literature Anthologies

Following is a list of anthologies of prose and poetry by Native Americans for general or adult audiences. Some content may not be suitable for younger readers.

American Indian Literature: An Anthology. Edited by Alan R. Velie. Norman: University of Oklahoma Press, 1979, 1991. 78021387. 90050700. 0806115300 hc. 0806115238 pb. 0806123451 pb. revised edition

Aniyunwiya/Real Human Beings: An Anthology of Contemporary Cherokee Prose. Edited by Joseph Bruchac. Greenfield Center, NY: Greenfield Review Press, 1995. 94078574. 0912678925 pb.

Dreams and Thunder: Poems, Stories, and The Sun Dance Opera by Zitkala-Sa. 2001027070. 0803249187 hc.

Durable Breath: Contemporary Native American Poetry. Edited by John E. Smelcer and D. L. Birchfield. Chugiak, AK: Salmon Run Press, 1994. 096340007X pb.

Earth Power Coming: Short Fiction in Native American Literature. Edited by Simon J. Ortiz. Tsaile, AZ: Navajo Community College Press, 1983. 83060959. 0912586508 pb.

Earth Song, Sky Spirit: Short Stories of the Contemporary Native American Experience. Edited by Clifford E. Trafzer. New York: Doubleday, 1993. 92044296. 0385469594 hc.

Growing Up Native in Alaska. Edited by A. J. McClanahan. CIRI Foundation, 2001. 1578331145 pb.

Growing Up Native American: An Anthology. Edited by Patricia Riley. Foreword by Inés Hernandez. New York: Morrow, 1993. Avon, 1995. 92046484. 068811850X hc. 0380724170 pb.

Harper's Anthology of 20th Century Native American Poetry. Edited by Duane Niatum. San Francisco: Harper & Row, 1988, 1999. 86045023. 006250665X pb. 0062506668 pb. 0613181166 lib. bdg. Econo-Clad.

Into the Moon: Heart, Mind, Body, Soul: The Native Women's Writing Circle. Edited by Lenore Keeshig Tobias. Toronto: Sister Vision Press, 1999. 1896705049 pb.

The Lightning Within: An Anthology of Contemporary American Indian Fiction. Edited by Alan R. Velie. Lincoln: University of Nebraska Press, 1991. 90012658. 0803246595 hc. 0803296142 pb. reprint edition.

The Magic World: American Indian Songs and Poems. Edited by William Brandon. New York: Morrow, 1971. 77153771. Athens: Ohio University Press, 1991. 90047852. 0821409816 hc. 0821409913 pb.

Malama, Hawaiian Land and Water. Edited by Dana Naone Hall. Honolulu: Bamboo Ridge Press, 1985. 85072888. 0910043124 pb.

Native American Literature: A Brief Introduction and Anthology. Edited by Gerald Vizenor. Berkeley: University of California, 1995. 95001693. 0673469786 pb.

Native American Literature: An Anthology. Edited by Lawana Trout. Lincolnwood, IL: NTC Pub. Group, 1999. 98038987. 0844259853 pb., student text. 0844259861 instructor's edition. 0613033248 lib. bdg.

Native American Reader: Stories, Speeches, and Poems. Edited by Jerry D. Blanche. Juneau, AK: Denali Press, 1990. 89016987. 0938737201 pb.

Native American Songs and Poems: An Anthology. Edited by Brian Swann. New York: Dover, 1997. 96024331. 0486294501 pb.

Native American Women's Writing: An Anthology, c.1800-1924. Edited by Karen Kilcup. Malden, MA: Blackwell Publishers, 2000. *Blackwell Anthologies* series. 99086315. 0631205179 hc. 0631205187 pb.

Neon Pow-Wow: New Native American Voices of the Southwest. Edited by Anna Lee Walters. Flagstaff, AZ: Northland, 1993. 93008947. 0873585623 pb.

New Voices from the Longhouse: An Anthology of Contemporary Iroquois Writing. Edited by Joseph Bruchac. Greenfield Center, NY: Greenfield Review Press, 1989. 87080178. 0912678682 pb.

Race with Buffalo and Other Native American Stories for Young Readers by Richard Young and Judy Dockrey Young. Little Rock: August House, 1994. 94006145. 0874833434 hc. 0874833426 pb.

Raven Tells Stories: An Anthology of Alaskan Native Writing. Edited by Joseph Bruchac. Greenfield Center, NY: Greenfield Review Press, 1991. 90085173. 0912678801 pb.

Reinventing the Enemy's Language: Contemporary Native Women's Writing of North America. Edited by Joy Harjo and Gloria Bird. New York: W. W. Norton & Company, 1997. 96036547. 0393040291 hc. 0393318281 pb.

The Remembered Earth: An Anthology of Contemporary Native American Literature. Edited by Geary Hobson. Albuquerque: University of New Mexico Press, 1979, 1981. 80054561. 0826305849 hc. 0826305687 pb.

Returning the Gift: Poetry and Prose from the First North American Native Writers' Festival. Edited by Joseph Bruchac. Tucson: University of Arizona Press, 1994. *Sun Tracks* series. 94004845. 0816513767 hc. 0816514860 pb.

Shaking the Pumpkin: Traditional Poetry of the Indian North Americas. Compiled by Jerome Rothenberg. Albuquerque: University of New Mexico Press, 1991. 90039916. 0826312462 pb. Previous editions 1972, Doubleday and 1986 A. van der Marck Editions.

Sister Nations: Native American Women Writers on Community. Edited by Heid E. Erdrich and Laura Tohe. Foreword by Winona LaDuke. St. Paul: Minnesota Historical Society Press, 2002. *Native Voices* series. 2001057986. 0873514270 hc. 0873514289 pb.

Songs from This Earth on Turtle's Back: Contemporary American Indian Poetry. Edited by Joseph Bruchac. Greenfield Center, NY: Greenfield Review Press, 1983. 82082420. 0912678585 pb.

Songs of the Tewa. Edited and translated by Herbert Joseph Spinden. Santa Fe, NM: Sunstone Press, 1993. 92033989. 0865341931 pb. Previous editions 1933 and 1976.

Tewa Poetry. Originally published for the Exposition of Indian Tribal Arts in New York in 1933.

Spider Woman's Granddaughters: Traditional Tales and Contemporary Writing by Native American Women. Edited by Paula Gunn Allen. Boston: Beacon Press, 1989. 88047655. 0807081000 hc. 044990508X pb.

Stories for a Winter's Night: Short Fiction by Native Americans. Edited by Maurice Kenny. Buffalo, NY: White Pine Press, 2000. 99088311. 1877727962 pb.

Talking Leaves: Contemporary Native American Short Stories. Edited by Craig Lesley. New York: Laurel/Dell, 1991. 92139334. 0440503442 hc. 0385312725 pb.

That's What She Said: Contemporary Poetry and Fiction by Native American Women. Edited by Reyna Green. Bloomington: Indiana University Press, 1984. 83049002. 0253358558 hc. 0253203384 pb.

Through the Eye of the Deer: An Anthology of Native American Women Writers. Edited by Carolyn Dunn and Carol Comfort. San Francisco: Aunt Lute Books, 1999. 99052696. 1879960583 pb.

Visit Teepee Town: Native Writings after the Detours. Edited by Diane Glancy and Mark Nowak. Minneapolis: Coffee House Press, 1999. 98052208. 1566890845 pb.

Voices of the Rainbow: Contemporary Poetry by American Indians. Edited by Kenneth Rosen. Illustrations by R. C. Gorman and Aaron Yava. New York: Viking, 1975. 75002374. 0670747572 hc. New York: Arcade, 1993, 1999. 93008517. 0805001875 pb. 0394177479 pb. 0785757465 lib. bdg. Econo-Clad.

Chapter 5

Nonfiction

Titles in this chapter are nonfiction books written specifically for young readers. Books and materials in this chapter cover a multitude of topics including biographies, celebrations, philosophy, religion, tribes, games, history, art, crafts, genealogy, ecology, speeches, outdoor life, nature, food, language, values, and more.

Some early-day American Indians who published nonfiction are Samson Occum (1723-1792); George Copway (1818-1869); Peter Jones, Kahkewaquonaby (1803-1856); Charles Warren (1825-1853); William Apes (1798- ?); Chief Andrew J. Blackbird (c. 1827-?); Chief Elias Johnson, Maungwudaus; George Henry; David Cusick; Peter Dooyentate Clarke; Mourning Dove, Christine Quintasket (1888-1936); Sarah Winnemucca Hopkins (1844?-1891); Emily Pauline Johnson (1861-1913); Alexander Lawrence Posey (1873-1908); John Milton Oskison (1874-1947); John Joseph Mathews (1894-1979); and Ella Cara Deloria (1888-1970).

Some other contemporary Native American nonfiction writers include Margaret Archuleta, Marilou Awiakta, Tiana Bighorse, D. L. Birchfield, Sam Blowsnake, E. K. Caldwell, Duane Champagne, Brenda Child, Ward Churchill, Leonard Crow Dog, Mary Crow Dog, Adam Fortunate Eagle, Janet Campbell Hale, Barbara Harjo, Ladonna Harris, George Horse Capture, Basil Johnson, Betty Mae Jumper, Juanita Tiger Kavena, Yeffe Kimball, Francis La Flesche, Julie Pearson Little Thunder, K. Tsianina Lomawaima, Wilma Mankiller, Russell Means, Vincent Mendoza, Devon Mihesuah, Earl Mills, Nasdijj, Leonard Peltier, Lynette Perry, Peter Razor, Delphine Red Shirt, Lawney L. Reyes, Anne Moore Shaw, Beverly Singer, John Stands in Timber, Leroy TeCube, Neal White, and Darryl Babe Wilson.

As Long as the Rivers Flow: The Stories of Nine Native Americans

Authors: Paula Gunn Allen and Patricia Clark Smith

Publication: New York: Scholastic, 1996

LC#: 95047642

Editions: 0590478699 hc.

Description: 334 pages, illustrated, 22 cm, bibliography, index

Subjects:

Indians of North America—Biography—Juvenile literature

Indians of North America—Kings and rulers—Juvenile literature

Indian women—North America—Biography—Juvenile literature

Interest Level: Grades 5-8

Reviewed: *Booklist*, *Kirkus*

Battlefields and Burial Grounds: The Indian Struggle to Protect Ancestral Graves in the United States

Author: Roger C. Echo-Hawk

Publication: Minneapolis: Lerner Publications, 1994

LC#: 92039893

Editions: 0822526638 lib. bdg.

Description: 80 pages, illustrated, 27 cm, map, bibliography, index

Interest Level: Grades 7-10, 7-12, young adult

Reading Level: 9.8

Summary: Describes the efforts of Native Americans to rebury ancestral human remains and grave offerings held by museums and historical societies, with particular emphasis on the Pawnees and their struggle to reclaim their dead.

Subjects:

Antiquities—United States—Law and legislation—Juvenile literature

Archaeology—Moral and ethical aspects—Juvenile literature

Human remains (Archaeology)—United States—Juvenile literature

Indians of North America—Funeral customs and rites—Juvenile literature

Indians of North America—Legal status, laws, etc.—Juvenile literature

Indians of North America—Religion—Juvenile literature

Indians of North America—Social life and customs

Tests: Accelerated Reader, Reading Counts

Lists: Oyate

Reviewed: *Booklist*, *Horn Book*, *Kirkus*, *School Library Journal*

Bowman's Store: A Journey to Myself

Author: Joseph Bruchac

Publication: New York: Dial Books, 1997; New York: Lee & Low Books, 2001

LC#s: 96033708 (Dial), 2001016435 (Lee & Low)

Editions: 0803719973 hc. (Dial), 1584300272 pb. (Lee & Low)

Description: 311 pages, illustrated, 24 cm (Dial); 315 pages, illustrated, 21 cm (Lee), 35 chapters

Interest Level: Young adult

Subjects:

Abenaki Indians—Biography

Abenaki Indians—Mixed descent

Bruchac, Joseph, 1941-

Indian authors—New York (State)—Biography

Lists: Notable Book in the Field of Social Studies National Council of Social Studies, International Reading Association

A Boy Called Slow: The True Story of Sitting Bull

Author: Joseph Bruchac

Illustrator: Rocco Baviera

Publication: New York: Philomel Books, 1994

LC#: 93021233

Editions: 0399226923 lib bdg., 069811616X pb.

Description: Picture book, 32 pages, color illustrations, 29 cm

Subjects:

Dakota Indians—Biography—Juvenile literature

Indians of North America—Biography

Kings, queens, rulers, etc.

Sitting Bull, 1834?-1890—Juvenile literature

Interest Level: Ages 4-8, 6-9

Reviewed: *Booklist, Horn Book*

A Braid of Lives: Native American Childhood

Editor: Neil Philip

Publication: New York: Clarion Books, 2000

LC#: 00021343

Editions: 039564528X hc.

Description: 84 pages, illustrated, 26 cm, bibliography, indexes

Summary: Weaves the testimony of many Native Americans into a single narrative of childhood and growing up.

Subjects:

Indian children—Biography—Juvenile literature

Indian philosophy—North America—Juvenile literature

Indians of North America—Biography—Juvenile literature

Interest Level: Grades 4-8, 4 and up

Reading Level: 5.0

Tests: Accelerated Reader

Reviewed: *Booklist, Horn Book, Kirkus, School Library Journal, VOYA*

Lists: ALA Best Books for Young Adults, *New York Times* Notable Book

Children of Clay: A Family of Pueblo Potters

Author: Rina Swentzell

Illustrator: Bill Steen

Publication: Minneapolis: Lerner Publications, 1992

Series: *We Are Still Here*

LC#: 92008680

Editions: 0822526549 lib. bdg., 082259627X pb.

Description: 48 pages, color illustrations, 22 × 25 cm, maps, bibliography, glossary

Summary: Members of a Tewa Indian family living in Santa Clara Pueblo in New Mexico follow the ages-old traditions of their people as they create various objects of clay.

Subjects:

Indians of North America—Social life and customs

Pottery craft—New Mexico—Santa Clara Pueblo—Juvenile literature

Santa Clara Pueblo (N.M.)—Social life and customs

Tewa Indians—Social life and customs—Juvenile literature

Chapter 5: Nonfiction

Tewa potters—Biography—Juvenile literature

Tewa pottery—Juvenile literature

Interest Level: Ages 9-12

Reading Level: 4.0

Tests: Accelerated Reader, Reading Counts

Reviewed: *Booklist*, *Horn Book*

Clambake: A Wampanoag Tradition

Author: Russell M. Peters

Illustrator: John Madama

Publication: Minneapolis: Lerner Publications, 1992

Series: *We Are Still Here*

LC#: 92008423

Editions: 0822526514 lib. bdg., 0822596210 pb.

Description: 48 pages, color illustrations, 22 × 25 cm, bibliography, glossary

Summary: Steven Peters, a twelve-year-old Wampanoag Indian in Massachusetts, learns from his grandfather how to prepare a clambake in the tradition of his people.

Subjects:

Clambakes—Massachusetts—Mashpee—Juvenile literature

Indians of North America—Massachusetts—Rites and ceremonies

Peters, Steven

Wampanoag Indians—Rites and ceremonies—Juvenile literature

Wampanoag Indians—Social life and customs—Juvenile literature

Interest Level: Ages 9-12

Reading Level: 5.0

Tests: Accelerated Reader, Reading Counts

Reviewed: *School Library Journal*

Lists: International Reading Association, Teacher's Choice

Note: Notable Children's Trade Book in Social Studies, Children's Book Council and National Council for Social Studies

Dat-so-la-lee: Artisan

Author: Gayle Ross

Publication: Parsippany, NJ: Modern Curriculum Press, 1994

LC#: 94077306

Editions: 0813657342 lib. bdg., 0813657407 pb.

Description: 40 pages, illustrated

Subjects:

Basket makers

Dat-so-la-lee, ca. 1829-1925—Biography—Juvenile literature

Indian baskets—Nevada—Juvenile literature

Indians of North America—Nevada—Biography

Washo baskets

Washo Indians—Biography—Juvenile literature

Women—Biography

Interest Level: Ages 4-8, 9-12

Day with a Pueblo = Giornata con un indiano Taos

Author: Tito E. Naranjo

Illustrator: Giorgio Bacchin

Publication: Minneapolis: Runestone Press, 2000

LC#: 98054143

Editions: 0822519194 lib. bdg.

Description: 48 pages, color illustrations, 31 cm, maps, bibliography, index

Summary: Describes a day in the life of a Pueblo elder.

Subjects:

Indians of North America—Southwest, New

Old age

Taos aged—Juvenile literature

Taos Indians—Social life and customs—Juvenile literature

Taos Pueblo (NM)—Social life and customs—Juvenile literature

Interest Level: Ages 9-12

Reading Level: 6.5

Tests: Accelerated Reader, Reading Counts

Reviewed: *Horn Book*

Notes: Bilingual—English and Spanish.

Drumbeat . . . Heartbeat: A Celebration of the Powwow

Author and Illustrator: Susan Braine

Publication: Minneapolis: Lerner Publications, 1995

Series: *We Are Still Here*

LC#: 94042594

Editions: 0822526565 lib. bdg., 082259711X pb.

Description: 48 pages, illustrated, 22 × 25 cm, bibliography, glossary

Subjects:

Indians of North America—Rites and ceremonies—Juvenile literature

Indians of North America—Social life and customs—Juvenile literature

Powwows—Juvenile literature

Interest Level: Ages 9-12, Grades 4-6

Reading Level: 6.8

Tests: Accelerated Reader, Reading Counts

Reviewed: *School Library Journal*

Enduring Wisdom: Sayings from North American Indians

Author: Virginia Driving Hawk Sneve

Illustrator: Paul Sneve

Publication: New York: Holiday House, 2003

LC#: 98038527

Editions: 0823414558 hc.

Summary: A collection of quotations from American Indians throughout the continent dated from the earliest contact with Europeans to contemporary tribal persons.

Subjects:

Indian philosophy—North America—Juvenile literature

Indians of North America—Quotations—Juvenile literature

First Americans Book series

Author: Virginia Driving Hawk Sneve

Illustrator: Ronald Himler

Publication: New York: Holiday House, 1994, 1997

Description: 32 pages, color illustrations, 24 × 26 cm, maps

LC#s and Editions: *The Apaches* 96041358. 0823412873 lib. bdg., *The Cherokees* 95024099. 0823412148 lib. bdg., *The Cheyennes* 95050696. 0823412504 lib. bdg., *The Hopis* 95001259. 082341194X lib. bdg., *The Iroquois* 94003748. 082341163 lib. bdg., *The Navajos* 92040330. 0823410390 lib. bdg., *The Nez Perce* 93038598. 0823410900 lib. bdg., *The Seminoles* 936014316. 082341125 lib. bdg., *The Sioux* 92023946. 0823411710 lib. bdg.

Subjects:

Apache Indians

Apache Indians—History—Juvenile literature
Apache Indians—Social life and customs—Juvenile literature
Cherokee Indians—Juvenile literature
Cheyenne Indians—Juvenile literature
Dakota Indians—Juvenile literature
Hopi Indians—History—Juvenile literature
Hopi Indians—Social life and customs—Juvenile literature
Indians of North America
Indians of North America—Great Plains
Indians of North America—New Mexico
Indians of North America—Southwest, New
Iroquois Indians—Juvenile literature
Navajo Indians—Juvenile literature
Nez Percé Indians—History—Juvenile literature
Nez Percé Indians—Social life and customs—Juvenile literature
Seminole Indians—Juvenile literature
Interest Level: Ages 5-8, 6-9, 9-12
Reading Level: *The Navajos* 4.0

Fort Chipewyan Homecoming: A Journey to Native Canada

Author: Morningstar Mercredi
Illustrator: Darren McNally
Publication: Minneapolis: Lerner Publications, 1997
Series: *We Are Still Here*
LC#: 96015786
Editions: 082252659X hc., 0822597314 pb.
Description: 48 pages, illustrated, 22 × 25 cm, map, bibliography, glossary
Summary: Twelve-year-old Matthew Dunn learns about the traditional ways of his Chipewyan, Cree, and Métis ancestors on a trip to Fort Chipewyan, in Alberta, Canada.

Subjects:
Chipewyan Indians—Social life and customs—Juvenile literature
Cree Indians—Social life and customs—Juvenile literature
Indians of North America—Canada—Social life and customs
Métis—Social life and customs—Juvenile literature
Interest Level: Ages 9-12
Reading Level: 4.7
Tests: Accelerated Reader

Four Seasons of Corn: A Winnebago Tradition

Author: Sally M. Hunter
Illustrator: Joe Allen
Publication: Minneapolis: Lerner Publications, 1997
Series: *We Are Still Here*
LC#: 96017625
Editions: 0822526581 lib. bdg., 0822597411 pb.
Description: 48 pages, color illustrations, 22 × 25 cm, map, bibliography, glossary
Summary: Twelve-year-old Russell learns how to grow and dry corn from his Winnebago grandfather.
Subjects:
Corn—Folklore
Corn—Social aspects—Juvenile literature
Indians of North America—Food
Winnebago Indians—Food—Juvenile literature
Interest Level: Ages 9-12, Grades 3-6
Reading Level: 5.5
Tests: Accelerated Reader
Reviewed: *Booklist*, *Horn Book*, *Kirkus*

Gift Horse: A Lakota Story

Author and Illustrator: S. D. Nelson
Publication: New York: Harry N. Abrams, 1999
LC#: 98051666
Editions: 0810941279 hc.
Description: Picture book, 40 pages, color illustrations, 27 cm
Summary: Relates the story of a Lakota youth whose father gives him a horse to prepare him for the transition from boyhood to manhood and becoming a Lakota warrior.
Subjects:
Dakota Indians
Dakota youth—Juvenile literature
Horses—Great Plains—Juvenile literature
Indians of North America—Great Plains
Interest Level: Grades 2-5
Reading Level: 3.0
Tests: Reading Counts
Reviewed: *Horn Book*, *Publishers Weekly*, *School Library Journal*
Lists: Oyate, Parents' Choice

Giving Thanks: A Native American Good Morning Message

Author: Chief Jake Swamp
Illustrator: Erwin Printup, Jr.
Publication: New York: Lee & Low Books, 1995
LC#: 94005955
Editions: 1880000156 hc., 1880000547 pb., 0613050614 lib. bdg. Econo-Clad
Description: Picture book, 24 pages, color illustrations, 29 cm
Subjects:
Human ecology—Juvenile literature
Mohawk Indians—Juvenile literature
Nature—Religious aspects—Juvenile literature
Speeches, addresses, etc. Mohawk—Juvenile literature
Interest Level: Ages 4-6, 4-8
Reading Level: 3.3
Tests: Accelerated Reader, Reading Counts.
Reviewed: *Booklist*, *Horn Book*, *Midwest Book Review*, *Publishers Weekly*, *School Library Journal*
Lists: Choices Cooperative Children's Book Center, Oyate, Reading Rainbow
Note: Available in Spanish translation.

God's Love Is Like

Author and Illustrator: Ray Buckley
Publication: Nashville, TN: Abingdon Press, 1998
LC#: 99173202
Editions: 0687056268 hc.
Description: 32 pages, illustrated, 24 cm
Summary: Multicultural stories relate five of the parables Jesus told.
Subjects:
Jesus Christ—Parables—Juvenile literature
Parables—Juvenile literature
Interest Level: Ages 4-8, 6-8
Reviewed: *Publishers Weekly*

Grandmother's Christmas Story: A True Quechan Indian Story

Author: Richard Red Hawk
Illustrator: Ross Coates
Publication: Sacramento, CA: Sierra Oaks Publishing, 1987
LC#: 88134817

Editions: 0940113082 pb.

Description: 39 pages, color illustrations, 20 × 22 cm

Subjects:

Christmas—Juvenile literature

Indians of North America—California—History—Juvenile literature

Yuma Indians—History—Juvenile literature

Interest Level: Ages 9-12

In a Sacred Manner I Live: Native American Wisdom

Editor: Neil Philip

Publication: New York: Clarion Books, 1997

LC#: 96006509

Editions: 0395849810 hc.

Description: 93 pages, illustrated, 27 cm, bibliography, indexes

Summary: A collection of speeches, or portions of speeches, made by Native Americans.

Subjects:

Human ecology—Native Americans—Philosophy—Juvenile literature

Indian philosophy—Native Americans—Juvenile literature

Indians of North America

Speeches, addresses, etc., Indian—North America—Juvenile literature

Interest Level: Ages 10 and up, Grades 3-7, 4 and up, young adult

Reading Level: 4.0

Tests: Accelerated Reader

Reviewed: *Booklist*, *Horn Book*, *Kirkus*, *New York Times*, *School Library Journal*

List: ALA Best Books for Young Adults

Indian Boyhood

Author: Charles Alexander Eastman

Illustrator: E. L. Blumenschein

Publication: New York: McClure, Philips & Company, 1902; New York: Dover, 1971

LC#: 68058282

Editions: 0486220370 pb.

Description: 255 pages, illustrated, 22 cm

Summary: A full-blooded Santee Sioux Indian describes his childhood experiences and training as a warrior in the late nineteenth century until he was taken to live in the white man's world at age fifteen.

Subjects:

Eastman, Charles Alexander, 1858-1939

Santee children—Juvenile literature

Santee Indians—Biography

Santee Indians—Social life and customs—Juvenile literature

Interest Level: Ages 8-12

Lists: Oyate

Note: This title may also be available from other publishers.

Indian Scout Craft and Lore

Author: Charles A. Eastman

Publication: Boston: Little, Brown, 1914. New York: Dover, 1974

LC#: 73090637

Editions: 0486229955 pb.

Description: 190 pages, illustrated, 21 cm, 26 chapters

Summary: A full-blooded Sioux trained as a warrior to age sixteen discusses the crafts, lore, and customs that were the essence of that training.

Subjects:

Boy Scouts—Juvenile literature

Camp Fire Girls—Juvenile literature

Indians of North America—Social life and customs—Juvenile literature

Outdoor life—Juvenile literature

Interest Level: Ages 4-8

Ininatig's Gift of Sugar

Author: Laura Waterman Wittstock

Illustrator: Dale Kakkak

Publication: Minneapolis: Lerner Publications, 1993

Series: *We Are Still Here*

LC#: 93037980

Editions: 0822526530 lib. bdg., 0822596423 pb.

Description: 48 pages, illustrated, 22 × 25 cm, map, bibliography, glossary

Summary: Describes how American Indians have relied on the sugar maple tree for food and tells how an Anishinabe Indian in Minnesota continues his people's traditions by teaching students to tape the trees and make maple sugar.

Subjects:

Indians of North America—Minnesota—Social life and customs

Maple sugar—Minnesota—Juvenile literature

Maple syrup—Minnesota—Juvenile literature

Ojibwa Indians—Social life and customs—Juvenile literature

Sugar maple—Tapping—Minnesota—Juvenile literature

Interest Level: Ages 9-12

Reading Level: 4.0

Tests: Accelerated Reader, Reading Counts

Reviewed: *Horn Book*

Note: Notable Children's Trade Book in the Field of Social Studies, NCSS/CBC

Itse Selu: Cherokee Harvest Festival

Author: Daniel Pennington

Illustrator: Don Stewart

Publication: Watertown, MA: Charlesbridge, 1994

LC#: 93027147

Editions: 0881068519 hc., 0881068527 lib. bdg., 0881068500 pb.

Description: 32 pages, color illustrations, 23 × 28 cm

Subjects:

Cherokee Indians—Rites and ceremonies—Juvenile literature

Cherokee Indians—Social life and customs—Juvenile literature

Harvest festivals—Southern States—Juvenile literature

Indians of North America

Interest Level: Ages 5-8, Grades K-3

Reading Level: 4.0

Tests: Accelerated Reader, Reading Counts

Reviewed: *Booklist*, *Horn Book*, *School Library Journal*

Lists: Notable Children's Trade Book in Social Studies, Oyate

Note: Includes an information page with a Cherokee syllabary and biographical information about Sequoyah.

Kinaaldá: A Navajo Girl Grows Up

Author and Illustrator: Monty Roessel

Publication: Minneapolis: Lerner Publications, 1993

Series: *We Are Still Here*

LC#: 92035204

Editions: 0822526557 lib. bdg., 0822596415 pb.

Description: 48 pages, color illustrations, 22 × 25 cm, bibliography, glossary

Summary: Celinda McKelvey, a Navajo girl, participates in the Kinaaldá, the traditional coming-of-age ceremony of her people.

Subjects:

Indians of North America—Southwest, New—Rites and ceremonies

Kinaaldá (Navajo rite)—Juvenile literature

McKelvey, Celinda—Juvenile literature

Navajo Indians—Biography—Juvenile literature

Navajo Indians—Rites and ceremonies—Juvenile literature

Puberty rites—New Mexico—Bloomfield—Juvenile literature

Interest Level: Ages 9-12, Grades 3-7, 4-7

Reading Level: 5.0

Tests: Accelerated Reader, Reading Counts

Reviewed: *Booklist*, *Horn Book*, *Kirkus*, *School Library Journal*

List: BCCB

Lakota Hoop Dancer

Author: Jacqueline Left Hand Bull

Illustrator: Suzanne Haldane

Publication: New York: Dutton Children's Books, 1999

LC#: 98021905

Editions: 0525454136 hc.

Description: 32 pages, color illustrations, 25 × 26 cm

Summary: Follow the activities of Kevin Locke, a Hunkpapa Indian, as he prepares for and performs the traditional Lakota hoop dance.

Subjects:

Hoop dance—South Dakota—Juvenile literature

Indians of North America—South Dakota

Teton Indians—Juvenile literature

Interest Level: Ages 9-12

Reading Level: 6.0

Tests: Accelerated Reader

Reviewed: *Booklist*, *Horn Book*, *Kirkus*

Lists: 2000 Notable Books for a Global Society, International Reading Association

Lasting Echoes: An Oral History of Native American People

Author: Joseph Bruchac

Illustrator: Paul Morin

Publication: San Diego, CA: Silver Whistle, 1997; New York: Avon Books, 1999

LC#s: 97011884 (Silver)

Editions: 015201327X hc. (Silver), 0380731843 pb. (Avon)

Description: 168 pages, illustrated, 24 cm bibliography

Summary: Discusses the history of Native Americans, with a sampling of excerpts from their own accounts of their experiences.

Subjects:

Indians of North America—History—Juvenile literature

Oral tradition—United States—Juvenile literature

Interest Level: Ages 9-12, Grades 7-12

Reading Level: 7.5

Tests: Accelerated Reader

Reviewed: *Horn Book*, *Kirkus*, *Publishers Weekly*, *School Library Journal*, *VOYA*

The Library of Intergenerational Learning Series

Titles: *Apache Children and Elders Talk Together*, *Blackfoot Children and Elders Talk*

Together, Crow Children and Elders Talk Together, Lakota Sioux Children and Elders Talk Together, Seminole Children and Elders Talk Together, Zuni Children and Elders Talk Together.

Author: E. Barrie Kavasch

Publication: New York: PowerKids, 1999

LC#s: 97049267 (Apaches), 98011834 (Blackfoot), 98022050 (Crow), 98033692 (Lakota), 97041100 (Seminole), 97049266 (Zuni)

Editions: all have lib. bdgs. 0823952258 (Apaches), 0823952282 (Blackfoot), 0823952312 (Crow), 0823952266 (Lakota), 0823952290 (Seminole), 0823952274 (Zuni)

Descriptions: 24 pages, color illustrations, 21 × 26 cm, indexes

Summaries:

Apaches: Explores the culture and traditions of the Apache people through the voices of Apache children and older people.

Blackfoot: Explores the culture and traditions of the Blackfoot people through the voices of some children and elders who are trying to maintain the customs of the past.

Crow: Explores the culture and traditions of the Crow Indians through the voices of a young girl, her father, and several other older people.

Lakota: Explores the land, culture, traditions, and current status of the Oglala Lakota Sioux on the Pine Ridge Reservation in South Dakota through the voices of a young girl and several elders.

Seminole: A child and older person of the Seminole Native American tribe of Florida talk about their history, culture, and festivals.

Zuni: Explores the culture and traditions of the Zuni people through the voices of their children and older people.

Subjects:

Apache Indians—Juvenile literature

Crow Indians—Juvenile literature

Indians of North America

Indians of North America—Florida—Juvenile literature

Indians of North America—Great Plains—Juvenile literature

Indians of North America—Montana

Indians of North America—New Mexico

Intergenerational relations—Great Plains—Juvenile literature

Oglala children—Juvenile literature

Oglala Indians—Social life and customs—Juvenile literature

Seminole Indians—Juvenile literature

Siksiska Indians—History—Juvenile literature

Siksiska Indians—Social life and customs—Juvenile literature

Zuni Indians—Juvenile literature

Reading Levels: 4.3-4.9

Tests: Accelerated Reader, Reading Counts

The Lumbee

Author: Adolph L. Dial

Publication: New York: Chelsea House Publishers, 1993

Series: *Indians of North America*

LC#: 92028917

Editions: 155546713X lib. bdg., 0791003868 pb.

Description: 112 pages, illustrated, 25 cm, bibliography, index

Subjects:

Lumbee Indians—Juvenile literature

Interest Level: Young adult

Many Nations: An Alphabet of Native America

Author: Joseph Bruchac

Illustrator: Robert F. Goetzl
Publication: Mahwah, NJ: BridgeWater Books, 1997
LC#: 97012271
Editions: 0816743894 hc., 0816744602 pb.
Description: 32 pages, color illustrations, 22 × 28 cm
Summary: Illustrations and brief text present aspects of the lives of the many varied native peoples across North America.
Subjects:
Alphabet
English language—Alphabet—Juvenile literature
Indians of North America—Juvenile literature
Indians of North America—Miscellaneous
Interest Level: Ages 4-8
Reviewed: *Horn Book*
Note: International Reading Association's Teacher's Choice Award

Maria Tallchief, Prima Ballerina

Author: Vee Browne
Publication: Parsippany, NJ: Modern Curriculum Press, 1994
Series: *Beginning Biographies*
LC#: 94077300
Editions: 0813657679 pb.
Subjects:
Ballerinas—United States—Biography—Juvenile literature
Ballet dancers
Indian ballerinas—United States—Biography—Juvenile literature
Indians of North America—Biography
Osage Indians—Biography
Tallchief, Maria—Juvenile literature
Women—Biography
Interest Level: Ages 4-8, 9-12

Meet Naiche: A Native Boy in Maryland

Author: Gabrielle Tayac
Illustrator: John Harrington
Publication: Hillsboro, OR: Beyond Words Publishing, 2002
Series: *My World—Young Native Americans Today*
LC#: 2002066651
Editions: 1582700729 hc.
Description: 48 pages, illustrated, map
Summary: Details a day in the life of a rural Maryland boy of Piscataway and Apache descent, looking at his family, the history of his tribe, and some traditional ceremonies and customs that are still observed today.
Subjects:
Apache Indians—Juvenile literature
Indians of North America—Maryland
Indians of North America—New Mexico
Piscataway Indians—Biography—Juvenile literature
Tayac, Naiche Woosah—Juvenile literature
Interest Level: Ages 9-12

The Mohawks of North America

Author: Connie Ann Kirk
Publication: Minneapolis: Lerner Publications, 2002
Series: *First Peoples*
LC#: 00012665
Editions: 0822548534 lib. bdg.
Description: 48 pages, color illustrations, maps, 27 cm, bibliography, glossary, index
Subjects:
Indians of North America
Mohawk Indians—Juvenile literature
Interest Level: Ages 9-12

Reviewed: *The Book Report*

Native American Games and Stories

Authors: James Bruchac and Joseph Bruchac
Illustrator: Kayeri Akweks
Publication: Golden, CO: Fulcrum Kids, 2000
LC#: 00010016
Editions: 1555919790 pb.
Description: 82 pages, illustrated, 23 cm, bibliography, index
Subjects:
Folklore—North America
Indians of North America—Folklore
Indians of North America—Games—Juvenile literature
Indians of North America—Social life and customs—Juvenile literature

Native People, Native Ways Series

Author: White Deer of Autumn
Illustrator: Shonto Begay
Publication: Hillsboro, OR: Beyond Words Pub., 1992
LC#s: Volume 1: 92012270; Volume 2: 92012269; Volume 3: 92017001; Volume 4: 92017002
Editions: Volume 1: 0941831426 pb., Volume 2: 0941831434 pb., Volume 3: 0941831736 pb., Volume 4: 0941831736 pb.
Descriptions: 88 pages, illustrated, 22 cm, bibliographies
Volume 1: *The Native American Book of Knowledge*. Explores the origins of the Native Americans and profiles key figures in the Americas before Columbus, including Deganawida, Hyonwatha, and others who have had a mystical and spiritual impact on the People.
Volume 2: *The Native American Book of Life*. Focuses on the Native Americans' life with the European settlers after Columbus and their attempt to retain their culture and traditions in a changing, modern world.
Volume 3: *The Native American Book of Change*. This third volume focuses on Native Americans' attempts over the centuries to retain their culture in the face of a changing world.
Volume 4: *The Native American Book of Wisdom*. A collection of stories focusing on the spiritual and medicine man traditions of the Native Americans.
Subjects:
Indian children—North America—Juvenile literature
Indians of North America—Ethnic identity
Indians of North America—Food—Juvenile literature
Indians of North America—History
Indians of North America—Juvenile literature
Indians of North America—Medicine—Juvenile literature
Indians of North America—Religion—Juvenile literature
Indians of North America—Social life and customs
Prejudices—Juvenile literature
Prophecies—Juvenile literature
Interest Level: Ages 4-8, young adult
Reading Level: Volume 2: 4.0
Tests: Volume 2: Reading Counts

Navajo ABC: A Dine Alphabet Book

Author: Tapahonso, Luci and Eleanor Schick
Illustrator: Eleanor Schick

Publication: New York: Macmillan Books for Young Readers, 1995

LC#: 94046881

Editions: 0689803168 hc., 0689826850 pb., 0613159225 lib. bdg. Econo-Clad

Description: Picture book, 32 pages, color illustrations, 29 cm

Subjects:

Alphabet

Navajo Indians—Juvenile literature

Navajo language—Glossaries, vocabularies, etc.—Juvenile literature

Interest Level: Ages 4-8, Grades K-3

Reading Level: 2.0

Reviewed: *Booklist, Horn Book, Kirkus, Publishers Weekly, School Library Journal*

Navajo Long Walk: The Tragic Story of a Proud People's Forced March from Their Homeland

Author: Joseph Bruchac

Illustrator: Shonto Begay

Publication: Washington, D.C.: National Geographic Society, 2002

LC#: 2001000567

Editions: 0792270584 hc.

Description: 54 pages, color illustrations, 28 cm, 7 chapters

Subjects:

Bosque Redondo Indian Reservation (NM)—Juvenile literature

Navajo Indians—History—Juvenile literature

Navajo Long Walk, 1863-1867—Juvenile literature

Interest Level: Ages 8-12, 9-12, Grades 4-8

Reviewed: *Booklist, Publishers Weekly*

Night Flying Woman: An Ojibway Narrative

Author: Ignatia Broker

Illustrator: Steven Premo

Publication: St. Paul: Minnesota Historical Society Press, 1983

LC#: 83013360

Editions: 0873511646 hc., 0873511670 pb., 0873512936 audio cassettes (3)

Description: 149 pages, illustrated, 23 cm

Summary: Contains accounts of the lives of several generations of Ojibway people in Minnesota and provides detailed information about their history and culture.

Subjects:

Indians of North America—Minnesota—History—Juvenile literature

Indians of North America—Minnesota—Social life and customs—Juvenile literature

Ojibwa Indians—History—Juvenile literature

Ojibwa Indians—Social life and customs—Juvenile literature

The Ojibway Dream

Author: Arthur Shilling

Publication: Montreal and Plattsburgh, NY: Tundra, 1986

LC#: 94198275

Editions: 0887764916 pb.

Description: Picture book, 48 pages, color illustrations, 31 cm

Subjects:

Indians of North America

Shilling, Arthur, 1941-1986

Interest Level: Ages 9-12

Lists: Oyate

The Pawnee Nation

Author: Anna Lee Walters
Publication: Mankato, MN: Bridgestone Books, 2000
Series: *Native Peoples*
LC#: 99053063
Editions: 073680501X lib. bdg.
Description: 24 pages, illustrated, 21 cm, map, bibliography, index
Summary: An overview of the past and present lives of the Pawnee Nation including their history, food and clothing, homes and family life, religion, music, and government.
Subjects:
Indians of North America—Great Plains
Pawnee Indians—History—Juvenile literature
Pawnee Indians—Social life and customs—Juvenile literature
Interest Level: Ages 4-8
Reading Level: 4.1
Tests: Accelerated Reader

People of the Buffalo: How the Plains Indians Lived

Author: Maria Campbell
Illustrators: Douglas Tate and Shannon Twofeathers
Publication: Vancouver: J. J. Douglas, 1976
Series: *How They Lived in Canada*
LC#: 79312763
Editions: 0888940890 hc., 088894396 pb., 0833596489 lib. bdg. Econo-Clad
Description: 47 pages, illustrated, 29 cm
Summary: Examines the self-sufficient existence of the Indian tribes living on the plains of the United States and Canada.
Subjects:
Indians of North America—Great Plains—Juvenile literature
Interest Level: Ages 9-12
Reading Level: 4.5
Tests: Reading Counts

The People Shall Continue

Author: Simon J. Ortiz
Illustrator: Sharol Graves
Publication: San Francisco, CA: Children's Book Press, 1977, 1988
LC#: 77083856, 88018929, rev. ed.
Editions: 0892390158 hc., 0892390417 lib. bdg. rev. ed., 0892391251 pb. rev. ed.
Description: 23 pages, color illustrations, 25 cm
Summary: Traces the progress of the Indians of North America from the time of the Creation to the present.
Subjects:
Indians of North America—History—Juvenile literature
Interest Level: Ages 9-12, Grades 3-7
Reading Level: 4.0
Tests: Accelerated Reader, Reading Counts
Reviewed: *Booklist, Five Owls, Horn Book, Multicultural Review, Publishers Weekly*

A Rainbow at Night: The World in Words and Pictures by Navajo Children

Author: Bruce Hucko
Publication: San Francisco: Chronicle Books, 1996
LC#: 96006861
Editions: 0811812944 hc.

Description: 44 pages, illustrated, 24 × 28 cm

Summary: Uses pictures in various mediums created by Navajo children to help explain Navajo culture and history. Suggests activities for the reader to do relating to family and feelings.

Subjects:

Activity programs in education—United States—Juvenile literature

Children's art—Juvenile literature

Indians of North America

Navajo children—Juvenile literature

Navajo Indians—Juvenile literature

Interest Level: Ages 9-12, Grades 4-6

Reading Level: 2.0

Reviewed: *Booklist, Horn Book, Skipping Stones*

Lists: Oyate

A River Lost

Author: Lynn Bragg

Illustrator: Virgil Marchand

Publication: Blaine, WA: Hancock House, 1995

LC#: none

Editions: 0888393830 pb.

Description: Picture book, 32 pages, color illustrations, 28 cm

Subjects:

British Columbia—Arrow Lakes Region—Juvenile literature

Grand Coulee Dam (Wash.)—Environmental aspects—Juvenile literature

Salmon—Effect of dams on—Juvenile literature

Salmon fisheries—British Columbia—Arrow Lakes Region—Juvenile literature

Interest Level: Ages 3-12

Sacajawea, Translator and Guide

Author: Irene Nakai Hamilton

Publication: Parsippany, NJ: Modern Curriculum Press, 1994

LC#: 94077298

Editions: 0813657598 hc., 0813657652 pb.

Description: 26 pages, color illustrations, 21 cm

Subjects:

Indians of North America—Biography

Lewis and Clark Expedition (1804-1806)—Juvenile literature

Sacagawea, 1786-1884—Juvenile literature

Shoshoni Indians—Biography—Juvenile literature

Women—Biography

Seasons of the Circle: A Native American Year

Author: Joseph Bruchac

Illustrator: Robert F. Goetzl

Publication: Mahwah, NJ: Troll/BridgeWater Books, 2002

LC#: 2002020013

Editions: 0816774676 hc.

Description: Picture book, 32 pages, color illustrations

Summary: Illustrations and brief text introduce activities of various Native American people in each month of the year.

Subjects:

Indians of North America—Social life and customs—Juvenile literature

Months

Seasons—Juvenile literature

Interest Level: Ages 4-8

Seeing the Circle

Author: Joseph Bruchac
Publication: Katonah, NY: R. C. Owen Publishers, 1999
Series: *Meet the Author*
LC#: 99025330
Editions: 1572743271 hc.
Description: 32 pages, illustrated, 24 cm
Summary: The author tells how he learned about his own Native American background, how he became a writer, and how he spends his days.
Subjects:
Abenaki Indians—Biography—Juvenile literature
Authors, American—20th century—Biography—Juvenile literature
Bruchac, Joseph, 1942—Juvenile literature
Children's stories—Authorship—Juvenile literature
Indian authors—United States—Biography—Juvenile literature
Indians of North America—New York (State)—Biography
Interest Level: Grades 2-5
Reading Level: 5.4
Tests: Reading Counts
Reviewed: *Library Journal, School Library Journal*

The Seminoles

Author: E. Barrie Kavasch
Publication: Austin, TX: Raintree Steck-Vaughn, 2000
Series: *Indian Nations*
LC#: 99028202
Editions: 0817254641
Description: 48 pages, illustrated, 26 cm, bibliography, index
Summary: Introduces the history, culture, and daily life of the Seminoles.
Subjects:
Indians of North America—Southern States
Seminole Indians—Juvenile literature
Interest Level: Ages 9-12, Grades 4-7
Reviewed: *School Library Journal*

Shannon: An Ojibway Dancer

Author: Sandra King
Illustrator: Catherine Whipple
Publication: Minneapolis: Lerner Publications, 1993
Series: *We Are Still Here*
LC#: 92027261
Editions: 0822526522. lib. bdg., 0822596431 pb.
Description: 48 pages, color illustrations, 22 × 25 cm, bibliography, glossary
Summary: A twelve-year-old Ojibwa Indian living in Minneapolis, Minnesota, learns about her tribe's traditional costumes from her grandmother and gets ready to dance at the powwow.
Subjects:
Indian dance—Minnesota
Indians of North America—Costume—Minnesota
Ojibwa dance—Juvenile literature
Ojibwa Indians—Costume
Ojibwa Indians—Rites and ceremonies—Juvenile literature
Powwows—Minnesota—Minneapolis—Juvenile literature
Interest Level: Ages 9-12, Grades 3-7
Reading Level: 3.0
Tests: Reading Counts
Reviewed: *School Library Journal*

The Shoshone

Author: Ned Blackhawk
Publication: Austin, TX: Raintree Steck-Vaughn, 2000
Series: *Indian Nations*
LC#: 99023347
Editions: 0817254684 lib. bdg.
Description: 48 pages, illustrated, 26 cm, bibliography, index
Summary: Introduces the history, culture, and daily life of the Shoshone Indians and examines the challenges they have faced since their first contact with Europeans.
Subjects:
Indians of North America
Shoshoni Indians—Juvenile literature
Interest Level: Ages 9-12

Songs from the Loom: A Navajo Girl Learns to Weave

Author: Monty Roessel
Publication: Minneapolis: Lerner Publications, 1995
Series: *We Are Still Here*
LC#: 94048765
Editions: 0822526573 lib. bdg., 082259711X pb., 0822597128 pb.
Description: 48 pages, color illustrations, 22 × 25 cm, bibliography, maps, glossary
Subjects:
Folklore—Arizona
Handweaving—Arizona—Kayenta—Juvenile literature
Indians of North America—Arizona—Folklore
Navajo Indians—Folklore
Navajo Indians—Social life & customs—Juvenile literature
Navajo textile fabrics—Arizona—Kayenta—Juvenile literature
Roessel, Jaclyn
Interest Level: Ages 9-12, Grades 3-7
Reading Level: 5.2
Tests: Accelerated Reader, Reading Counts
Reviewed: *Booklist*, *Horn Book*, *School Library Journal*

A Story to Tell: Traditions of a Tlingit Community

Author: Richard D. Nichols
Illustrator: D. Bambi Kraus
Publication: Minneapolis: Lerner Publications, 1998
Series: *We Are Still Here*
LC#: 97009592
Editions: 0822526611 lib. bdg.
Description: 48 pages, illustrated, map, 22 × 25 cm, bibliography
Summary: An eleven-year-old Tlingit girl travels to Kake, Alaska, where she learns about her family's heritage from stories her grandmother tells.
Subjects:
Indians of North America—Alaska
Tlingit Indians—Juvenile literature
Interest Level: Ages 9-12

A Student's Guide to Native American Genealogy

Author: E. Barrie Kavasch
Publication: Phoenix, AZ: Oryx Press, 1996
Series: *Oryx American Family Tree*
LC#: 96010196
Editions: 0897749758 hc.

Description: 192 pages, illustrated, 24 cm, map, bibliography, index

Subjects:

Indians of North America—Genealogy—Handbooks, manuals, etc.

North America—Genealogy—Handbooks, manuals, etc.

Interest Level: Young adult

Reviewed: *Book News, Inc.*, *Children's Bookwatch*, *Midwest Book Review*

This Land Is My Land

Author: George Littlechild

Publication: Emeryville, CA: Children's Book Press, 1993

LC#: 93012932

Editions: 0892391197 lib. bdg.

Description: 30 pages, illustrated, 32 cm

Summary: Using text and his own paintings, the author describes the general experiences of North American Indians as well as his own experiences growing up as a Plains Cree Indian in Canada.

Subjects:

Cree Indians—Biography—Juvenile literature

Cree Indians—Social life and customs—Juvenile literature

Indians of North America

Littlechild, George—Juvenile literature

Interest Level: Ages 9-12, grades 6-9

Reviewed: *Booklist*, *Horn Book*, *Kirkus*

The Tiny Warrior: A Path to Personal Discovery & Achievement

Author: D. J. Vanas

Publication: Colorado Springs, CO: Native Discovery, 2001; Kansas City, MO: Andrews McMeel, 2003

LC#: none

Editions: 0971600007 pb.

Description: 96 pages, 19 cm, 10 chapters

Subjects:

Conduct of life

Indians of North America—Youth

Values

Youth—Conduct of life

Interest Level: Young adult

The Trail of Tears

Author: Joseph Bruchac

Illustrator: Diana Magnuson

Publication: New York: Random House, 1999

Series: *Step into Reading*

LC#: 98036199

Editions: 0679990526 lib. bdg., 0679890521 pb., 061322518X lib. bdg. Econo-Clad

Description: 46 pages, color illustrations, 24 cm

Summary: Recounts how the Cherokees, after fighting to keep their land in the nineteenth century, were forced to leave and travel 1200 miles to a new settlement in Oklahoma, a terrible journey known as the Trail of Tears.

Subjects:

Cherokee Indians—History—19th century—Juvenile literature

Cherokee Indians—Relocation—Juvenile literature

Indians of North America—Southern States—History

Trail of Tears, 1838—Juvenile literature

Interest Level: Ages 9-12

Reading Level: 4.8

Tests: Accelerated Reader, Reading Counts

Visions of the Buffalo People

Author: Linda Little Wolf
Publication: Plainwell, MI: Syncopated Press, 1999, 2000
LC#s: 99065164, 00101724
Editions: 0967197848 pb.
Description: 68 pages, 28 cm
Summary: The acquisition of the horse from Spanish explorers transformed the life and culture of the Plains Indians.
Subjects:
Horses—History
Indians of North America—History
Interest Level: Ages 9-12
Note: Includes projects, crafts, puzzles, recipes, and games.

Wampum Belts of the Iroquois

Author: Tehanetorens, Ray Fadden
Publication: Summertown, TN: Book Publishing Company, 1999
LC#: 99033789
Editions: 157067082X pb.
Description: 128 pages, illustrated, 23 cm
Summary: Describes the nature and significance of Indian wampum belts, focusing on their history and uses by the Iroquois.
Subjects:
Indians of North America—Social life and customs
Iroquois Indians—Social life and customs—Juvenile literature
Wampum belts—Juvenile literature
Interest Level: Ages 9-12

We Rode the Wind: Recollections of Nineteenth-Century Tribal Life

Editor: Jane B. Katz
Publication: Minneapolis: Lerner Publications, 1975, 1995
LC#: 74011909 (first ed.), 94034946 rev. ed.
Editions: 0822506394 (first ed.), 0822531542 lib. bdg. (rev. ed.)
Description: 110 pages (first ed.), 128 pages, illustrated, 23 cm bibliography, index
Subjects:
Indians of North America—Biography—Juvenile literature
Indians of North America—Juvenile literature
Contents: C. A. Eastman, J. Stands in Timber, Two Leggings, W. W. Warren, Waheenee, J. Whitewolf, and Black Elk.
Tribes: Cheyenne, Sioux, Ojibwa, and others
Reviewed: *Booklist*, *Horn Book*

Weaving a California Tradition: A Native American Basketmaker

Author: Linda Yamane
Illustrator: Dugan Aguilar
Publication: Minneapolis: Lerner Publications, 1997
Series: *We Are Still Here*
LC#: 96013388
Editions: 0822526603 lib. bdg., 0822597306 pb.
Description: 48 pages, illustrated, 22 × 25 cm, bibliography, glossary

Summary: Follows an eleven-year-old Western Mono Indian as she and her relatives prepare materials needed for basketweaving, make the baskets, and attend the California Indian Basketweavers Association's annual gathering.

Subjects:

Basket making—California—Juvenile literature

Indians of North America—California

Mono baskets—Juvenile literature

Mono Indians—Social life and customs—Juvenile literature

Reading Level: 6.0

Tests: Accelerated Reader

Words of Wisdom for Children: Na 'Olelo No 'eau No Na Keiki

Authors: Lilia Wahinemaika'i Hale and Kimo Armitage

Illustrator: Solomon Enos

Publication: Waipahu, Hawaii: Island Heritage Publishing, 2001

LC#: none

Editions: 0896104648 hc.

Description: Picture book, 28 pages, color illustrations, 24 cm, pronunciation guide

Subjects:

Hawaiian culture—Juvenile literature

Philosophy of life—Juvenile literature

Note: Bilingual — English and Hawaiian

Yaqui Coloring Book: A Yaqui Way of Life

Author and Illustrator: Stan Padilla

Publication: Summertown, TN: Book Publishing Company, 1999

LC#: 00265840

Editions: 1570670684 pb.

Description: 29 pages, illustrated, 28 cm

Summary: Introduces the culture and beliefs of an ancient people from northwestern Mexico, now also in Arizona, through line drawings and brief text.

Subjects:

Coloring books

Indians of Mexico

Yaqui Indians—Juvenile literature

Chapter 6

Resources

Although the books in this chapter will be of particular interest to teachers and librarians, parents and students of Native American literature may also find them interesting.

Readers are encouraged to consult the Oyate site <www.oyate.org>, a useful resource that provides information on workshops, teacher materials, Oyate publications (some of which are listed in this chapter), books to avoid, book recommendations (preschool through high school), recommended reference materials, audios, videos, posters, and more.

The Web site of the Council for Indian Education <www.cie-mt.org/> has information on teacher training and "culturally authentic" reading and instructional materials. The Native American books section of the Native American Indian Resources Web page <www.kstrom.net/isk/books/bookmenu.html> contains a number of evaluative reviews by Paula Giese. Lisa Mitten, a Native American librarian, provides valuable resource information on her site <www.nativeculture.com/lisamitten/indians.html>.

Cynthia Leitich Smith's excellent site <www.cynthialeitichsmith.com> on Children's Literature Resources contains bibliographies of Native American authors and artists, contemporary and historical fiction, an overview of Native American literature, and a teachers' and librarians' section with lesson plans, teacher guides, and more.

Earth Maker's Lodge: Native American Folklore, Activities, and Foods edited by E. Barrie Kavasch. Peterborough, NH: Cobblestone Publishing, 1994. 95118991. 0942389093 pb. 159 pages, illustrated, index. 1995 Book Builder's of Boston Award. A collection of histories, stories, legends, poems, folklore, games, activities, projects, and recipes from Cobblestone publications.

The Encyclopedia of the First Peoples of North America edited by Rayna Green and Melanie Fernandez. Toronto: Douglas & McIntyre/Groundwood, 1999. 0888993803 hc. Includes bibliography and index. 220 pages, illustrated.

How to Teach about American Indians: A Guide for the School Library Media Specialist by Karen D. Harvey with Lisa D. Harjo and Lynda Welborn. Westport, CT: Greenwood Press, 1995. 95009305. 0313292272 hc. 221 pages, bibliography, index. *Greenwood Professional Guides in School Librarianship* series.

How to Tell the Difference: A Guide to Evaluating Children's Books for Anti-Indian Bias by Beverly Slapin, Doris Seale, and Rosemary Gonzales. Cover illustration by John Kahionhes Fadden. Berkeley, CA: Oyate, 2000. 0962517550 pb. 27 pages, illustrated. Available from Oyate.

Igniting the Sparkle: An Indigenous Science Education Model by Gregory A. Cajete. Skyland, NC: Kivaki Press, 1999. 99073307. 1882308662 pb. 233 pages, illustrated, bibliography. Study and teaching of science.

Keepers of Life: Discovering Plants through Native American Stories and Earth Activities for Children by Michael J. Caduto and Joseph Bruchac. Illustrated by John Kahionhes Fadden, David Kanietakeron Fadden, Marjorie C. Leggitt, and Carol Wood. Golden, CO: Fulcrum Publishing, 1994. 94012584. 1555911862 pb. 265 pages, illustrated, indexes, glossaries, bibliography. 1555912141 audio cassette.

Keepers of the Animals: Native American Stories and Wildlife Activities for Children by Michael J. Caduto and Joseph Bruchac. Illustrated by John Kahionhes Fadden, David Kanietakeron Fadden, D. D. Tyler, and Carol Wood. Golden, CO: Fulcrum, 1997. 97022401. 1555913865 pb. 266 pages, illustrated, indexes, glossary. 1555911285 audio cassettes (2).

Keepers of the Earth: Native American Stories and Environmental Activities for Children by Michael J. Caduto and Joseph Bruchac. Illustrated by John Kahionhes Fadden and Carol Wood. Golden, CO: Fulcrum, 1997. 97022411. 1555913857 pb. 209 pages, illustrated, index, glossary. 1555910998 audio cassettes (2).

Keepers of the Night: Native American Stories and Nocturnal Activities for Children by Michael J. Caduto and Joseph Bruchac. Illustrated by David Kanietakeron Fadden, Jo Levasseur, and Carol Wood. Golden, CO: Fulcrum Publishing, 1994. 94002602. 1555911773 pb. 146 pages, illustrated, index, glossary. National Parenting Publications Award 1999.

Native American Gardening: Stories, Projects and Recipes for Families by Michael J. Caduto and Joseph Bruchac. Illustrations by Mary Adair, Adelaide Murphy Tyrol, and Carol Wood. Golden, CO: Fulcrum Publishing, 1996. 95047301. 155591148X pb. 158 pages, illustrated, map, bibliography, index.

The Native American Look Book: Art and Activities from the Brooklyn Museum by Missy Sullivan, Dawn Weiss, and

Barbara Zaffran. New York: The New Press, 1996. 95036245. 1565840224 pb. 48 pages, illustrated, bibliography.

Based on a program created by Dorothea Basile. Introduces Native American art and culture by examining a Kwakiutl whale mask, a Zuni water jar, and a Pomo basket at the Brooklyn Museum.

Navajo Native Dyes: Their Preparation and Use by Nonabah G. Bryan and Stella Young. Mineola, NY: Dover Publications, 2002. 2002018819. 0486421058 pb. 62 pages.

Power and Place: Indian Education in America by Vine Deloria, Jr. and Daniel R. Wildcat. Golden, CO: Fulcrum Resources, 2001. 2001001721. 155591859X pb. bibliography, index. 168 pages. 15 chapters.

Reclaiming the Vision: Past, Present, and Future: Native Voices for the Eighth Generation. Edited by Lee Francis and James Bruchac. Greenfield Center, NY: Greenfield Review Press, 1996. 95081637. 0878861408 pb. 153 pages.

Based on a July 1992 Returning the Gift conference of North American Native writers, who made encouraging Native American youth a goal.

Teaching about Native Americans by Karen D. Harvey, Lisa D. Harjo, and Jane K. Jackson. Washington, D.C.: National Council for Social Studies, 1998. 97068403. 0879860731 pb. 82 pages.

Teaching American Indian History by Terry P. Wilson. Washington, D.C.: American Historical Association, 1993. 93072224. 0872290697 pb. *Diversity within America* series. 66 pages. Bibliography.

Thanksgiving: A Native Perspective by Doris Seale, Beverly Slapin, and Carolyn Silverman. Cover illustration by John Kahionhes Fadden. Berkeley, CA: Oyate, 1995, 1998. pb. 101 pages, illustrated.

Available from Oyate. Material may be reproduced for classroom use only. Includes essays, stories, speeches, student activities, and teacher materials about stereotypes.

Three Strands in the Braid: A Guide for Enablers of Learning by Paula Underwood. Edited by Sarah Ann Robertson and Jeanne Lamar Slobod. Illustrated by Anne McDonald. San Anselmo, CA: Tribe of Two Press, 1994. 91065523. 1879678004 pb. 76 pages, illustrated, bibliography. Written to use with Underwood's *Who Speaks for Wolf, Winter White and Summer Gold*, and *Many Circles, Many Paths*.

Through Indian Eyes: The Native Experience in Books for Children edited by Beverly Slapin and Doris Seale. Los Angeles, CA: American Indian Studies, University of California, 1998. 98060445. 0935626468 pb. 253 pages, illustrated. Includes bibliography and index. Available from Oyate and elsewhere.

Chapter 7

Authors and Illustrators

In the interest of brevity, editors and compilers have not been included. For those individuals of mixed heritage, the non-Native ethnic heritages are not listed in this guide.

Dugan Aguilar (Maidu, Pit River, Paiute) is a photographer. He is from Susanville, California. Aguilar specializes in photographing California Native Americans. <www.wheelwright.org/lowry/aguilar.html>

Kayeri Akweks (Upper Mohawk) has worked as an art teacher and illustrator. Her special areas of art are Native American and Celtic history, traditions, and mythology. She lives in Ontario. <www.asfa-art.org/gallery/akweks.html>

Joe Allen is a photographer. His photographs illustrate *Four Seasons of Corn*.

Paula Gunn Allen (Sioux, Laguna Pueblo) grew up in New Mexico. She has taught at a number of universities. Her writings include a novel, poetry, and nonfiction. <http://voices.cla.umn.edu/Authors/PaulaGunnAllen.html#bookcover>

Dan Andreasen has illustrated *Eagle Song* by Joseph Bruchac, *Streets of Gold* by Rosemary Wells, and a number of other children's books. He lives in Medina, Ohio with his wife and children.

Author **Kimo Armitage** (native Hawaiian) grew up in Haleʻiwa, Oʻahu. He was raised by his grandparents. Memories of spearing fish, collecting rock salt, and picking limu provide Armitage with background for his writing.

Jose Aruego and **Ariane Dewey** are the illustrators of *How Chipmunk Got His Stripes*. Aruego grew up in the Philippines and worked as a lawyer there before coming to the United States to attend art school. He lives in New York City. Dewey grew up in Chicago. These two illustrators work together to create their illustrations.
<www.eduplace.com/kids/hmr/mtai/aruego_dewey.html>

Dennis Asato is the author and illustrator of several children's books. He is also a musician, computer technologist, and psychologist.

Te Ata, 1895-1995, (Chickasaw) was an internationally-known actress and storyteller. She performed at the White House and for British royalty. Eleanor Roosevelt named Lake Te Ata in New York state after her. In 1957 she was named to the Oklahoma Hall of Fame. Her life and career are featured in the video, *God's Drum* (Weststar Communications, 1995), and a play by Judy Lee Oliva.<www.ipl.org/div/natam/bin/browse.pl/A212>

Joy S. Au (Hawaiian) is the author of four nonfiction children's books. She grew up on the island of Kaua'i with her husband and son and now lives and works on O'ahu.

Mary Azarian, illustrator of *When the Moon Is Full*, received a Caldecott Medal in 1999 for her illustrations of *Snowflake Bentley*. She lives in Vermont.

Giorgio Bacchin is the illustrator of the *Day With* series from Runestone Press.

Rocco Baviera has illustrated a number of books including *A Boy Called Slow*.
<www.eduplace.com/kids/hmr/mtai/baviera.html>

Shonto Begay (Navajo) has authored and illustrated a number of books of award-winning picture books. He lives in Kayenta, Arizona with his family.

James Bernardin has illustrated a number of books including *Grandmother Spider Brings the Sun*. He lives in Huntington Beach, California.

Ned Blackhawk (Shoshone) is a professor of history at the University of Wisconsin, Madison. Blackhawk received the Huggins-Quarles Award from the Organization of American Historians.

Charles L. Blood is the co-author of *The Goat in the Rug* by Geraldine. According to the book's jacket, Blood is part American Indian.

E. L. Blumenschein was the illustrator of *Indian Boyhood* by Charles A. Eastman.

DuWayne (Duce) Leslie Bowen (Seneca) lives on the Allegany Reservation at Jimersontown-Salamanca, New York. He is a descendent of John O'Baill, the Cornplanter, a principal chief of the Seneca. Bowen and his family were forced to leave his home in the 1960s when the Kinzua Dam was constructed on the Allegany River.

Author **Linda Boyden** (Cherokee) is a member of the United Lumbee Nation. She is a storyteller in the field of American Indian myths. Boyden works in schools with writing projects for children. Originally from Massachusetts, she now lives in Hawaii with her husband. *The Blue Roses* is her first book.

Lynn Bragg (Colville) is the author of *A River Lost* and *Remarkable Idaho Women*. She grew up on Mercer Island, attended the University of Washington, and worked as a teacher on the Colville Reservation in Eastern Washington.

Author and illustrator **Susan Braine** (Assiniboine) was born in Montana and grew up on the Northern Cheyenne Reservation. She has managed radio stations in several states and is manager of American Indian Radio on Satellite. Braine is a photographer and a writer in Lincoln, Nebraska. <www.nativeamericacalling.org/nac_staffbios.shtml#susan>

Ignatia Broker, 1919-1987, (Ojibwe) was born in Minnesota. She worked as a teacher and curriculum developer at several schools. She was responsible for a number of stories, filmstrips, and booklets on Indian culture. Broker was also a researcher and active participant in many organizations. <http://voices.cla.umn.edu/authors/IgnatiaBroker.html>

Vee Browne (Diné) is the author of several books. She was born in Ganado, Arizona. Browne has earned a number of awards including a Cowboy Hall of Fame Award. She is a teacher and counselor at a school on the Navajo Reservation in Arizona.

James Bruchac (Abenaki) is a storyteller, teacher, author, and tracker. The son of Joseph Bruchac, he lives in Greenfield Center, New York, and is director of the Ndakinna Wilderness Project. <www.ndakinna.com/james.html>

Joseph Bruchac, Sozap (Abenaki) is the author of poetry, novels, and nonfiction and the founder of Greenfield Review Press. He lives in Greenfield Center, New York. Bruchac has received numerous awards including an American Book Award, a Cherokee Nation Prose Award, and Yaddo Residency Fellowships.
<www.eduplace.com/kids/hmr/mtai/bruchac.html>
< www.fulcrum resources.com/html/bruchac.html>

Ray Buckley (Lakota, Tlingit) is the author and illustrator of several picture books. He is also Director of Native American Ministries of United Methodist Communications.

S. S. Burrus, **Nannehi Tolese Siam** (Cherokee) has exhibited her artwork in shows around the world. She illustrated *The Girl Who Married the Moon* and other books. <http://home.earthlink.net/~intertribalartmarket/ITAMv3/SSBurrus/SSBurrus.html>

Maria Campbell (Métis) is best known for her autobiography, *Halfbreed*, in which she wrote about the bleak existence of her early life in Canada. Campbell has worked as a teacher and storyteller and was Writer-in-Residence at the University of Saskatchewan. <www.library.csi.cuny.edu/users/lavender/389/noframes/metis.html>

Christopher Canyon, illustrator of *Did You Hear Wind Sing Your Name?* and several other books, is a native of Columbus, Ohio, where he grew up and now lives with his wife. Canyon won the 1996 Benjamin Franklin Award for best picture book for *The Tree in the Ancient Forest*. <www.morleylibrary.org/Kids/Pava/chriscanyon.htm>

Illustrator **Beth Clark** (Seneca) is a member of the Deer Clan of the Seneca Nation. She grew up in New York state and lives in Salamanca, New York. Clark has been recognized for her art.

Verna Clinton (Navajo) is an author, illustrator, and a teacher at Chinle Elementary School on the Navajo Nation. She has illustrated a number of children's books and books about Navajo life.

Ross Coates has illustrated several children's books including *Grandfather's Maidu Indian Tales*, *Grandfather's Story of Navajo Monsters*, and *When Hopi Children Were Bad*. Coates has experience teaching art at Washington State University and lives in Pullman, Washington. <www.wsu.edu/~finearts/faculty/coates/index.htm>

Tom Coffin (Potawatomi, Creek) is the illustrator of *Coyote in Love with a Star*. Originally from Kansas, Coffin is a painter and sculptor and works in architectural restoration. He now lives in Arizona. <www.art.net/Studios/Visual/Coffin/coffin.html>

Amy Córdova is an author as well as an artist. She is the art director of an arts based elementary school. She lives in Ranchos de Taos, New Mexico.

Francis Cree, **Eagle Heart** (Ojibway) is an elder and storyteller. He lives in North Dakota, where he is recognized as a healer, leader, and storyteller.

Gerald Dawavendewa (Hopi, Cherokee) is the author and illustrator of *The Butterfly Dance*. Dawavendewa works at the Lunar and Planetary Laboratory at the University of Arizona in Tucson and is also a teacher.

Sandra De Coteau Orie (Oneida) is the author of *Did You Hear Wind Sing Your Name?* She is also recognized for her work in the field of poetry.

Martha Kreipe De Montaño (Potawatomi) is the author of *Coyote in Love with a Star* and co-author of *The Native American Almanac*. She is manager of the Resource Center of the National Museum of the American Indian, Manhattan Branch. Originally from Kansas, she lives in New York. <http://staff.lib.muohio.edu/nawpa/DeMontano.html>

Brian Deines is an artist and photographer. The illustrator of *Skysisters and Bear on the Train*, Deines lives in Toronto, Ontario.

Adolph Lorenz Dial, ?-1995, (Lumbee) was the author of *The Lumbee* and *The Only Land I Know: A History of the Lumbee Indians*. Dial, Professor Emeritus at the University of North Carolina at Pembroke, was the first chairman of the American Indian Studies Department there. A building and scholarship at the university bear his name.

Kim Doner is an illustrator and designer. She is the illustrator of several picture books.

Michael Dorris, 1945-1997, (Modoc) was the founder of the Native American Studies program at Dartmouth College. He was awarded the National Book Critics Circle Award in 1989 for *The Broken Cord*, a nonfiction account of his adopted son's fetal alcohol syndrome. Dorris married Louise Erdrich in 1981, and they collaborated on several books. Dorris wrote both fiction and nonfiction for children and adults.

Charles A. Eastman, Ohiyesa, 1858-1939, (Dakota Sioux) was raised in a traditional manner by his grandparents. He attended several colleges including Dartmouth and Boston University Medical School. A licensed physician, he offered aid to victims of the Wounded Knee massacre in 1890. Eastman worked for the Y.M.C.A. to provide programs for Indian children. A storyteller and writer, he wrote several guides for the Boy Scouts and Camp Fire Girls. <www.kstrom.net/isk/stories/authors/eastman.html>

Roger C. Echo-Hawk (Pawnee) is a co-author of *Battlefields and Burial Grounds*. He is a scholar, historian, and professor at the University of Colorado in Boulder.

Walter R. Echo-Hawk (Pawnee) graduated from the University of New Mexico with a law degree. He is the co-author of *Battlefields and Burial Grounds*. Echo-Hawk received the Spirit of Excellence Award from the American Bar Association in 1996.

Anthony Chee Emerson (Navajo) is an artist and a commercial painter. He has an art gallery in Farmington, New Mexico, which features the work of his artistic family. <www.emersongallery.com/about.htm>

Illustrator **Solomon Enos** (native Hawaiian) grew up in Hawaii. Because his family did not have television, he developed his love for art. Enos now lives and farms in Hawaii.

Lise Erdrich (Ojibway) works as a counselor and teacher in Wahpeton, North Dakota. *Bears Make Rock Soup* is her first children's book.

Louise Erdrich (Chippewa) grew up in North Dakota. She attended Dartmouth College and Johns Hopkins University. Erdrich is the author of poetry, novels, and nonfiction for children and for adults. <www.english.uiuc.edu/maps/poets/a_f/erdrich/erdrich.htm>

Ron Evans (Chippewa, Cree, Assiniboin) grew up in Montana and western Canada. He is a storyteller. <www.ipl.org/cgi/ref/native/browse.pl/A253>

Carolyn (C. S.) Ewing is the illustrator of *Rabbit's Wish for Snow*.

David Kanietakeron Fadden (Mohawk) is the illustrator of *Native Plant Stories*, *Keepers of Life*, *Native American Stories*, and other books. With his father and other family members, he operates the Six Nations Indian Museum in Onchiota, New York.

John Kahionhes Fadden (Mohawk) is an illustrator of *Native Plant Stories*, *The Faithful Hunter*, and other books. He is director of the Six Nations Indian Museum in Onchiota, New York, a storyteller, and a teacher. <www.thebeadsite.com/MUS-F4.htm>

Lisa Fifield (Oneida) is a well-known watercolor artist and quilt maker. Fifield grew up in California and Washington and now lives and works in Minnesota. <www.arcticravengallery.com/lisafifield.html>

Teresa Flavin is the illustrator of *Pushing Up the Sky*. <www.kji.co.uk/pages/teresa.htm>

Stephen Gammell is the author and illustrator of a number of books. He has received three Caldecott or Caldecott Honor Medals for his illustrations. <www.bookpage.com/0006bp/stephen_gammell.html>

Robert F. Goetzl illustrated *Many Nations* and *Seasons of the Circle*.

Sharol Graves (Shawnee) is the illustrator of *The People Shall Continue*. Graves has combined computer technology with Native designs in her work as an artist.

Carol Grigg is the illustrator of *The Great Change*. Her prints, t-shirts, and posters are available at a variety of sources on the Internet. <www.beyondword.com/authors/griggc.html>

Suzanne Haldane is a photographer. Her photographs are featured in *Lakota Hoop Dancer*. She is also the author of several books for children.

Chaika Piilani Hale (native Hawaiian) grew up in Honolulu. She has taught in public and private schools in California and Hawaii. She has two children.

Author **Lilia Wahinemaika'i Hale** (native Hawaiian) enjoys her life on the Waimanalo Homestead. She is the mother of five, grandmother of 24, and great grandmother of 80!

Joy Harjo (Muskogee-Creek) is an author, poet, and lead vocalist and saxophone player for Poetic Justice. She received a Lifetime Achievement Award from the Native Writers Circle. A member of the advisory board of *Red Ink* magazine, she lives in Honolulu.
<www.hanksville.org/storytellers/joy/>
<www.unm.edu/~wrtgsw/harjo.html>
<http://voices.cla.umn.edu/authors/JoyHarjo.html>

Irene Nakai Hamilton (Navajo) is the author of *Sacajawea, Translator and Guide*.

John Harrington is a photographer in Washington, D.C. His photographs illustrate *Meet Naiche*. <www.johnharrington.com/>

Beatrice O. (Orcutt) Harrell (Choctaw) is the author of *How Thunder and Lightning Came To Be* and *Longwalker's Journey*.

Storyteller **Vi Hilbert** (Upper Skagit) has been honored as a Washington state living treasure. Hilbert is founder and director of Lushootseed Research, an organization for preserving her tribal heritage. <www.ipl.org/div/natam/bin/browse.pl/A155>

Illustrator **Ronald Himler** attended Cleveland Institute of Art and Cranbrook Academy of Art in Bloomfield, Michigan. He lives in Tucson, Arizona.

Allan C. Houser, Haozous, 1914-1994, (Chiricahua Apache) was the illustrator of *Runner in the Sun*. Originally from Oklahoma, Houser was a teacher and a well-known artist. Exhibitions of his artistic works and sculpture traveled to Europe.
<www.allanhouserfoundation.org/main.html>

Gregg Howard (Cherokee, Powhatan) was named Storyteller of the Year by the Wordcraft Circle of Native writers and storytellers. He lives in Texas.
<http://hometown.aol.com/vipublish/Kanohesgiaol.html>

Frank Howell provided artwork for Paul Underwood's *Who Speaks for Wolf*. Howell is a well-known artist in Santa Fe, New Mexico. <www.frankhowellgallery.com/>

Bruce Hucko is a photographer and the author of *A Rainbow at Night* and *Where There Is No Name for Art*. He conducts teacher workshops and art residencies across the country.
<www.westfolk.org/voy/behindbruce.htm>

Sally M. Hunter (Anishinabe, Ojibway) is the author of *Four Seasons of Corn*. She is married to a Hochunk Indian and is a mother and grandmother. She lives in St. Paul, Minnesota. <www.turtle-tracks.org/issue41/i41_8.html>

Murv Jacob (Cherokee) is the illustrator of many books. He is also a painter and a pipe maker. He lives in Tahlequah, Oklahoma with his four children and his wife. <www.lakesok.com/lakesok/lakesoktk/LTKV0413.htm>

Rudy James, ThlauGooYailthThlee (Tlingit) is an author and illustrator, storyteller, lecturer, tribal spokesman, activist, and historian. He was born in southeast Alaska. He serves as judge for two tribal courts and was a leader in a case in which two Indian youth were banished to remote tribal lands. He is a director of the International Human Rights Association of American Minorities (IHRAAM), a part of the United Nations. <http://home.earthlink.net/~wolfhouse/author.html>

Rodney Johnson (Lakota Sioux) grew up in South Dakota. *The Secret of Dead Man's Mine* is his first novel. He lives in Los Angeles and writes for ZoogDisney.com. <www.uglytown.com/publishing/authors/rodneyjohnson.html>

Dale Kakkak (Menominee) is a book illustrator and a staff photographer for a native newspaper in Twin Cities. He is a poet as well as a fiction writer.

Scott Kaneshiro has illustrated four picture books. He was born and raised on the island of O'ahu. Since childhood, he has enjoyed fishing, golfing, spending time with family and friends, and art.

E. (Elizabeth) Barrie Kavasch (Creek, Cherokee) is an author, ethnobotanist, storyteller, food historian, and trustee and research associate at The Institute for American Indian Studies in Connecticut. <http://ebarriekavasch.hypermart.net/>

Geri (Geraldine) Keams (Navajo) is a storyteller, poet, and the author of *Grandmother Spider Brings the Sun* and *Snail Girl Brings the Water*. An Arizona native, she presents workshops on Native American storytelling. <www.monettech.com/paces/keams.html>

Sandra King (Ojibway) is a member of the Red Lake band of Ojibway. King has worked as an editor and a writer. She lives in St. Paul, Minnesota with her husband and their four children.

Thomas King (Cherokee) is a teacher, writer, photographer, and performer. He grew up in northern California. He was chairman of American Indian studies at the University of Utah. As the author of short stories and novels, King has received numerous awards for his writing. He lives in Ontario. <www.nwpassages.com/bios/king.asp>

Connie Ann Kirk (Seneca) is a writer and scholar. She and her husband and two sons live in the Finger Lakes area of New York.

D. (Denise) Bambi Kraus (Tlingit) grew up in the Seattle, Washington area. She is a freelance photographer and continues to be involved in national Indian policy issues.
<www.achp.gov/thpo.html>
<www.theprogressive.org/mpvdbk00.htm>

Michael Lacapa (Apache, Hopi, Tewa) is an artist and writer. His books include *The Mouse Couple*, *The Flute Player*, and *Antelope Woman*. He lives with his wife and children in Taylor, Arizona. With his wife Kathleen, he wrote *Less Than Half, More Than Whole*.
<www.ipl.org/cgi/ref/native/browse.pl/A304>

Illustrator **Paul Lee** attended college in Pasadena, California. A freelance illustrator and painter, he illustrated *Amistad Rising* by Veronica Chambers. Lee lives in Fullerton, California with his wife. <www.eduplace.com/kids/hmr/mtai/plee.html>

Jacqueline Left Hand Bull (Lakota) is the author of *Lakota Hoop Dancer*. She lives in Ontario where she is a counselor and leader of Baha'i.

Chief Lelooska, **Don Smith** (Cherokee) adopted into the Kwakiutl Nation, was a storyteller, carver, painter, and teacher. In 1998 he was awarded the Washington state Governor's Writers Award.

Martin Link, co-author of *The Goat in the Rug*, publishes *The Indian Trader* magazine.

Linda Little Wolf (Cherokee, Lakota Sioux) grew up in Long Island, New York. An educator and lecturer, she shares information about Plains Indian history, culture, and horsemanship. Little Wolf and her horse, Enough Stuff, have appeared in schools and fairs in the Southeast. She lives in Florida. <http://hometown.aol.com/nativevisions8>

George Littlechild (Cree, Micmac) is an author and illustrator. He was born in Edmonton, Alberta and now lives in British Columbia. Littlechild is the author of *This Land Is My Land* and has illustrated several picture books by Native American authors. His artwork is well known in Canada. <www.willockandsaxgallery.com/twillock/littlec1.htm>

Thomas Locker has illustrated a number of books including several by Joseph Bruchac. Locker attended the University of Chicago and now lives in Stuyvesant, New York with his family, which includes five sons. His artwork has been exhibited in several countries.

Michael Lomatuway'ma (Hopi) is the narrator of *The Magic Hummingbird*, an authentic folktale which is an example of Hopi oral literature.

Jonathan London is a co-author of *Fire Race* and *Thirteen Moons on Turtle's Back*. He has authored a large number of children's books. London lives with his family in California.
<www.eduplace.com/kids/hmr/mtai/london.html>

Sylvia Long is the illustrator of *Fire Race*.

Oren R. Lyons, **Joagquisho**, **Bright Sun** is a chief of the Onondaga Nation and a professor at the State University of New York at Buffalo. Lyons has been active in numerous causes on behalf of Native Americans.
<www.cicngo.org/orenbio.html>
<www.ratical.com/many_worlds/6Nations/OLatUNin92.html>
<www.ratical.com/co-globalize/OrenLyons.html>

John Madama is a photographer, writer, and desktop publisher. The owner of North Atlantic Graphics, he teaches computer publishing and visual design at Harvard, MIT, and Radcliffe College. He has worked as a designer, editor, video producer, and photographer. Madama lives and works in Gloucester, Massachusetts.

Illustrator **Jim Madsen** is responsible for the cover and interior illustrations of *Indian Shoes* by Cynthia Leitich Smith.

Diana Magnuson, illustrator of *The Trail of Tears*, has illustrated more than seventy books.
<www.kidsbooklink.org/magnuson.html>

Virgil "Smoker" Marchand (Colville) is the illustrator of *A River Lost* by Lynn Bragg. He is a member of the Arrow Lakes Band of the Colville Confederated Tribes.

Dea Marks illustrated *Little Fish*.

Linda R. Martin (Navajo) is the illustrator of *Brave Wolf and the Thunderbird*. She worked as communications manager for Atlatl, a service organization for Native American arts before becoming associate editor for *Native Peoples* magazine.

Author **Elaine McLeod** (Na-Cho Nyak Dun) was born in Mayo, Yukon. She has worked in many areas as a teacher. *Lessons from Mother Earth* is her first book. She and her husband have four children. Her stories were told to her children to help them understand their history and roots. She lives in Whitehorse, Yukon.

Darren McNally is an illustrator, photographer, and consultant. He is a native of Alberta, Canada, and lives in Edmonton, Alberta with his family.

D'Arcy McNickle, 1904-1977, (Salish, Kootenai) was born in Montana. He was the director of the Center for American Indian History in Chicago. A writer, activist, historian, and professor of anthropology, McNickle wrote several books of fiction and nonfiction.
<www.ipl.org/div/natam/bin/browse.pl/A49>

Joe Medicine Crow (Crow) is the author of *Brave Wolf and the Thunderbird* and *From the Heart of Crow Country*. He is a World War II veteran and is tribal historian.

Tony Meers is the illustrator of *Longwalker's Journey* and several other children's books.

Morningstar Mercredi (Athabaskan, Chipewyan, Cree, Métis) is a storyteller, television reporter, actress, consultant, and researcher. She lives with her son in Edmonton, Alberta.

Randy Messer is the illustrator of *Great Eagle and Small One*.

Ralph Moisa, Jr. (Yaqui) is an author, musician, and storyteller. He is the author of *Little Fish* and *Great Eagle and Small One*. Moisa lives in upstate New York with his wife and family.

N. Scott Momaday (Kiowa) is an author and a professor of literature at the University of Arizona in Tucson. Momaday was born in Oklahoma but grew up in Navajoland. He received the Pulitzer Prize in 1969 for *House Made of Dawn*, his first novel. Momaday is an artist as well as a writer.
<www.ipl.org/div/natam/bin/browse.pl/A50>
<www2.truman.edu/vscholar/mom-award.html>

Natachee Scott Momaday (Cherokee) is a writer, teacher, and artist. She was born in Kentucky. Her ancestry includes French, English, and Cherokee. In 1968, she received the Zia Award as the outstanding woman writer of New Mexico by the Press Women of New Mexico.
<www.ipl.org/cgi/ref/native/browse.pl/A5>

William Kent Monkman is the illustrator of *Coyote Columbus*.

Joel Monture, Teionhehkwen (Mohawk) is an author of several novels and an editor of *Multicultural Review*. From Ohsweken, Ontario, he was a professor of traditional Native arts at the Institute of American Indian Arts in Santa Fe, New Mexico. He has been recognized as a traditional artist and bead worker. Monture lives in Madison, Wisconsin.

Paul Morin has illustrated a number of children's books and twice received the Amelia Frances Howard-Gibbon Illustrator's Award and numerous other Canadian book awards.

Lynn Moroney (Chickasaw) is the author of *Baby Rattlesnake*, told by Te Ata. She is a storyteller and presents programs across the country. Moroney is the author of several books.
<http://title3.sde.state.ok.us/literatureanda/lynn.htm>

Johnny Moses (Nootka, Saanich, Snohomish, Dwamish, Chehamus) is a storyteller, spiritual leader, and healer. He was born on Vancouver Island, British Columbia, and has trained under seven traditional medicine teachers. He speaks nine languages.
<www.johnnymoses.com/lowres/index.html>

Beatrice Culleton Mosionier (Métis) was born in Winnipeg, Manitoba. The author of a number of books for children and adults, she lives in Toronto. Her book *April Raintree* is considered a classic of Native Canadian literature.

Tito E. Naranjo (Santa Clara Pueblo) is an artist and the author of *Day with a Pueblo*. He lives in New Mexico.

S. D. Nelson (Lakota) is an author and artist. A member of the Standing Rock Sioux, he attended Moorhead State University in Minnesota. Nelson teaches art in a middle school in Flagstaff, Arizona. <www.crizmac.com/SpeakerSeries.html>

Richard Nichols (Tewa Pueblo) is a writer and educator. From the Santa Clara Pueblo in New Mexico, Nichols has been an educational consultant for numerous educational endeavors. He lives in Washington, D.C.

Simon J. Ortiz (Acoma Pueblo) is a native of Acoma Pueblo in New Mexico. His writings include short stories, essays, and poetry. Ortiz is the author of more than thirty books.
<www.wwnorton.com/naal/explore/ortiz.htm>
<www.uwm.edu/Dept/Library/special/exhibits/nativelt/ho.htm#ORTIZ>

Stan Padilla (Yaqui) is a writer and artist. He is the author and illustrator of *Song of the Seven Herbs*, *A Natural Education*, *Deer Dancer*, *Dream Feather*, and others.

Nancy Winslow Parker is the illustrator of *The Goat in the Rug*, *Oh, A-Hunting We Will Go*, *Willy Bear* and other picture books. <www.nwparker.com/biog.htm

Daniel Pennington (Cherokee) is a freelance writer. He lives in Belmont, Massachusetts. He wrote *Itse Selu* to teach his daughter, Isadora, about her culture.

Don Perceval is the illustrator of *Owl in the Cedar Tree* by Natachee Scott Momaday.

Russell M. Peters (Wampanoag) grew up in Mashpee, Massachusetts, spent time in the U.S. Army, earned degrees from Morgan College and Harvard University, and worked in the computer industry and for the Coalition of Eastern Native Americans. In 1974, he became president of Mashpee Wampanoag Indian Tribal Council. He was project director of *People of the First Light*, a series of films about New England Native Americans.

Daniel Pheasant, **Spotted Horse** (Cherokee) was born in North Carolina. He is a storyteller, musician, dancer, and traditional craftsman and carver. He and his wife are the parents of two children. The family lives on the Qualla Boundary Indian Reservation in North Carolina.

Driver Pheasant (Cherokee) is a storyteller, musician, and Cherokee language teacher. He works at the Museum of the Cherokee Indian in Cherokee, North Carolina. He lives with his family on the Qualla Boundary Indian Reservation.

Lanny Pinola (Pomo, Miwok) is a dance artist, educator, and storyteller. He was born on the Kashaya reservation and grew up listening to stories of the elders. A graduate of Brigham Young University, Pinola is active in providing programs about his heritage.
<www.turtletrack.org/Issues00/Co10072000/CO_10072000_Storyteller.htm>

Penny Pollock (Wyandotte) is the author of a number of books for children. She was born in Cleveland, Ohio and grew up in Pennsylvania. A Quaker, she is the mother of four children. She and her husband spend their time in Brookside, New Jersey, Lake Owasco, New York, and Sarasota, Florida. <http://home.att.net/~penny-stewpollock/>

Steven Premo is the illustrator of *Night Flying Woman*.

Erwin Printup, Jr. (Cayuga, Tuscarora) is an artist. He was born in Niagara Falls, earned a fine arts degree from the Institute of American Indian Art in Santa Fe, New Mexico, and now lives in Lewiston, New York. *Giving Thanks* is his first picture book.
<http://infoweb.magi.com/~apikan/biographies/erwinbio.html>

Karen Reczuch has illustrated several award-winning books. She lives with her family in Acton, Ontario.

Richard Red Hawk (Wyandot) is the author of several fiction and nonfiction books for children. His books include *Grandmother's Christmas Story*, *Grandfather's Story of Navajo Monsters*, and *A Trip to a Pow Wow*.

Veg Reisberg illustrated *Baby Rattlesnake*, *Uncle Nacho's Hat*, and *Erlinda Who Danced in the Sky*.

Monty Roessel (Navajo) is a writer and photographer. He graduated from the University of Northern Colorado and has worked as a newspaper photographer, editor, and freelance photojournalist. His photographs have appeared in *Time*, *Newsweek*, *Arizona Highways*, *Sports Illustrated*, and numerous other publications. <www.kstrom.net/isk/maps/rugmap.html>

Gayle Ross (Cherokee) is an author and storyteller. She is the author and co-author of a number of children's books. She lives with her husband and children in Texas.
<www.classactsarts.org/artists/gaylepg.html>
<www.thegrand.com/details/gayle_ross.htm>

Susan L. Roth has illustrated a number of children's books including *The Great Ball Game*. She lives on the East Coast. <www.eduplace.com/kids/hmr/mtai/roth.html>

Daniel San Souci is an artist and illustrator of several children's books. He lives in Oakland, California with his wife and their children.

Eleanor Schick is the illustrator and co-author of *Navajo ABC*. An artist, Schick lives in Albuquerque, New Mexico. <www.nmcn.org/artsorgs/writersguide/schick.html>

Greg Shed has illustrated a number of books by several authors. He lives in San Diego, California. <www.salzmaninternational.com/pgs/GShed.html>

Arthur Shilling, 1941-1986, (Ojibway) was an author, illustrator, and artist. He was born in Ontario. The paintings for *The Ojibway Dream* were completed before his death.
<www.ilap.com/laparetegallery/shilling.htm>
<http://collections.ic.gc.ca/artists/shilling.html>

Duncan Sings-Alone (Cherokee) is a storyteller, an author, and a healer. He has worked as a minister and as a psychologist. <www.twocanoespress.com/duncan.html>

Cynthia Leitich Smith (Muscogee Creek) is the author of three books for young readers. Leitich Smith has worked in journalism, public relations, and law. She and her husband live in Austin, Texas. She maintains an excellent Web site for multicultural literature.
<www.harperchildrens.com/catalog/author_xml.asp?authorID=18584>

Patricia Clark Smith (Micmac) is the author and co-author of several books that include poetry and folklore. A professor of English, Smith teaches Native American literature.
<http://weberstudies.weber.edu/archive/Vol.%2016.2/patriciaclarksmith.html>

Paul Sneve (Sioux) is the illustrator of *Enduring Wisdom*. Sneve graduated from the University of South Dakota with a fine arts degree in 1983.

Virginia Driving Hawk Sneve (Rosebud Sioux) is the author of a number of books. A teacher, counselor, and a writer, she lives in South Dakota. Sneve was recognized with a National Humanities Medal in 2000.
<http://voices.cla.umn.edu/authors/VirginiaDrivingHawkSneve.html>
<www.yourexpedition.com/umbrella_pages/stories/s_w_jan8.html>

Bill Steen is a book illustrator, photographer, and consultant. His fields of interest include culture, environment, and community development. His photographs have appeared in numerous magazines and books. He and his wife, Athena, from the Santa Clara Pueblo, live in Canelo, Arizona. <www.caneloproject.com/pages/who.html>

Shirley Sterling (Niakapmux) is an author. She was born on the Joyaska Indian Reserve in British Columbia and trained as a classical ballerina. Sterling has received the Native Indian Teacher Education Alumni Award twice and a Laura Steinman Award for children's literature.
<www.groundwoodbooks.com/authors/ssterling.htm>

Don Stewart is an illustrator and a freelance artist. He earned a degree in fine arts from the University of North Carolina and now lives in Greensboro. <www.donstewart.com/>

Virginia A. Stroud (Cherokee) grew up in Oklahoma and was adopted into a Kiowa family after becoming an orphan at age eleven. An author and illustrator, Stroud is the author of *A Walk to the Great Mystery* and *Doesn't Fall Off His Horse* and has illustrated several books including *The Story of the Milky Way* and *The Path of Quiet Elk*. She is a former Miss Indian America. <http://title3.sde.state.ok.us/literatureanda/virginia.htm>

Chief Jake Swamp, **Tekaronianeken** (Mohawk) is an author. He was born on the Akwesasne Mohawk Reservation in New York. He is a founder of the Tree of Peace Society, an international organization that promotes peace and conservation. <www.treeofpeace.org/>

Rina Swentzell (Santa Clara Pueblo) is a writer, educator, and potter. She grew up in New Mexico and has taught at several universities in New Mexico, New York and California. Swentzell served as a consultant for the public television series *NOVA* and the Smithsonian Institution's Museum of the American Indian. She lives in New Mexico.

Luci Tapahonso (Navajo) is an author and professor at the University of Arizona and lives in Shiprock, New Mexico. She has received a Mountains and Plains Booksellers Association's Poetry Award, a Kansas Governor's Arts Award, a Distinguished Woman Award from the National Association of Women in Education, and has been featured in a poetry CD and several films. <http://voices.cla.umn.edu/authors/LuciTapahonso.html>

Douglas Tate is the illustrator of *People of the Buffalo*.

Tawa Mana, **Sun Girl** (Hopi, Tewa) is a coauthor of *When Hopi Children Were Bad*.

Gabrielle Tayac (Piscataway) is an author from a multicultural family. Her mother is Jewish and her father is Native American. She is married to a man from Colombia and their son is truly multicultural. Tayac works at the National Museum of the American Indian in Washington, D.C.

C. J. Taylor (Mohawk) is an artist as well as an author. Taylor was born in Montreal. Her father is Mohawk of the Deer Clan and her mother is German-British. Her works have been exhibited in the United States and Canada. Her books have been translated into Danish, Swedish, and French. The mother of three children, she lives in Canada.

Tchin (Blackfoot, Narragansett) was born in Norfolk Virginia. He is a musician, artist, folklorist, entertainer, and the author of *Rabbit's Wish for Snow*. He lives in New Jersey and is available for performances. <http://hometown.aol.com/tchinart/bio.htm>

Tehanetorens, **Ray Fadden** (Mohawk) lives in Onchiota, New York. He is a teacher and storyteller. With his family, he takes care of the Six Nations Indian Museum.

Dovie Thomason (Sickles) (Kiowa, Apache, Lakota) is a storyteller. She has participated in numerous storytelling conferences, workshops, and festivals sharing Native American stories. <www.yaconn.org/dovie_thomason.htm>

Jill Thompson is the illustrator of *The Secret of Dead Man's Mine*. She is the author of the *Scary Godmother* series. Thompson lives in Chicago.

Tim Tingle (Choctaw) is a storyteller and a workshop presenter. Tingle is also a musician, specializing in the Indian flute. He lives in Canyon Lake, Texas and operates Storytribe Publishing. <http://talesandlegends.net/direct.html#Tingle>

Douglas Poʻoloa Tolentino (Hawaiian) is an illustrator, artist, and musician. *Hawaiʻi Sings* is his first picture book. He lives on Oʻahu with his wife and daughter.

Gerald Rancourt Tsonakwa (Abenaki) is a storyteller originally from Quebec, Canada. He is a stone carver and sculptor. He and his wife, who is also an artist, share their art in tours across the U.S. and Canada. <www.gocaia.org/Artists/T/Tsonak/tsonak.htm>

Shannon Twofeathers is the illustrator of *People of the Buffalo*.

Paula Underwood, ? – 2000, (Oneida) was a storyteller, teacher, speaker, and writer. She developed a program called Learning Way, an educational program used in various organizations. To her came the responsibility for learning and passing on the oral tradition that had been passed down for five generations in her family.

Richard Van Camp (Dogrib) is the author of *What's the Most Beautiful Thing You Know about Horses?* <www.richardvancamp.org/>

Cornelius Van Wright and **Ying-Hwa Hu** are co-illustrators of a number of picture books including *Jingle Dancer*. They live and work in New York City. <www.cynthialeitichsmith.com/auth-illHuVanWright.htm>

D. J. Vanas, **Eagle Bear** (Odawa) is an author, motivational speaker, and trainer. Vanas has experience as a Sun Dancer, U.S. Air Force officer, and business owner. He lives in Colorado Springs, Colorado with his wife and daughter. <www.nativediscovery.com/>

George Vann, **Tsatsi** (Cherokee) is a storyteller from Oklahoma. During his retirement, Vann spends time visiting schools and telling stories.

Dietrich Varez (Hawaiian) is the author and illustrator of *Maui, the Mischief Maker*. Varez is a well-known artist in a variety of mediums including glass. <www.dublclick.com/coconutinfo/varez.html>

Pablita Velarde Tse Tsan (Santa Clara Pueblo, Tewa) was born in 1918 in Santa Clara Pueblo in New Mexico. During her long career as an artist, Velarde has defied traditions and acted as an advocate for Native women in the field of art. She continues to live in Santa Clara Pueblo. <www.artcyclopedia.com/artists/velarde_pablita.html>

Felix Vigil (Jicarilla Apache, Jemez Pueblo) is an artist and illustrator. He attended the Maryland Institute College of Art and has taught at the Institute of American Indian Arts in Santa Fe, New Mexico. Vigil lives in Jemez Pueblo in New Mexico. <www.abbeville.com/booktemplate.asp?stockno=1631>

Anna Vojtech is the illustrator of *The First Strawberries*. She lives in Marblehead, Massachusetts. <www.avojtech.com/>

Jan Bourdeau Waboose (Nishinawbe Ojibway) is the author of several books for children. She grew up in Northern Ontario. Her writing includes poetry and short stories that have been published in newspapers, magazines, and anthologies.

Johnny Wales has illustrated several picture books and is part of a Kodo drumming ensemble. A native of Toronto, he and his wife live in Japan.

Anna Lee Walters (Pawnee, Otoe-Missouria) was born and raised in Pawnee, Oklahoma. She has worked as a library technician, a curriculum developer and in the field of public relations. Walters has written in many genres including fiction, poetry, and nonfiction. She won an American Book Award in 1986. She and her husband and sons live in Arizona. <http://voices.cla.umn.edu/authors/annaleewalters.html>

Carson Waterman (Seneca) is an illustrator and artist. A member of the Snipe Clan of the Seneca Nation, he studied art in Cleveland, Ohio. His art has been exhibited in the northeastern United States. <www.nativeartvision.com/>

Sherrin Watkins (Shawnee) is the author of two children's books. She is a lawyer in Okmulgee, Oklahoma.

James Watling is an illustrator and a retired associate professor at McGill University. Watling lives near Montreal, Canada.

Catherine Whipple (Lakota) is a freelance photographer. A native of South Dakota, she is on the board of directors of Native Arts Circle in Minnesota. In 1991, she received a fellowship for her work in photographing children in Central America. She lives in Minneapolis. <www.thecirclenews.org/about.html>

White Deer of Autumn, **Gabriel Horn** (Narragansett, Wampanoag) is the author of several books. He has been a teacher, poet, curriculum developer, and cultural arts director at the Minneapolis American Indian Center. He lives in St. Petersburg, Florida, with his wife and their three children. <www.beyondword.com/authors/autumnw.html>
<www.redcloudindianarts.com/g-horn.htm>

Baje Whitethorne, Sr. (Navajo) is an author and illustrator of several books about Navajo culture. Whitethorne is originally from Shonto, Arizona. He is active in visiting schools. <http://salinabookshelf.com/Biographies/BajeWhitethorne/BajeBioPage.htm>

Maria Williams (Tlingit) is the author of *How Raven Stole the Sun*. She is the Native Folk Arts Director of the Alaska Council on the Arts. Williams has a doctorate in ethnomusicology and has taught at the University of New Mexico.
<www.ciri.com/newsletter/august2001/news.html>
<www.unm.edu/~finearts/about/publications/2000/2000profiles.htm>

Mary Louise Defender Wilson, **Gourd Woman** (Dakotah, Hidatsa) is a storytelling elder from North Dakota. <www.nwhp.org/tlp/biographies/wilson/wilson_bio.html>

Laura Waterman Wittstock (Seneca) is an author who has written about women, politics, and public policy. She has worked in radio communications, written for a newspaper, and edited and published newsletters. She is founder of MIGIZI Communications in Minneapolis. <http://migizi.org/mig/default.html>

Colleen Wood is an illustrator, graphic designer, and artist. Wood illustrated *Letters from Mother Earth*. She lives in Vancouver, B.C.

Linda Yamane (Rumsien Ohlone) is an author, artist, basket weaver, storyteller, and scholar in California. She has published a book of folklore, a book on native California plants, and *Weaving a California Tradition*. <www.oyate.com/linda.htm>

Author and illustrator **Leo Yerxa** (Ojibwe) was born on the Little Eagle Reserve in northern Ontario. An artist, Yerxa works in a variety of media. He has worked with the Royal Ontario Museum and the Canadian Museum of Civilization. He now lives in Ottawa and works as an artist. <www.groundwoodbooks.com/illustrators/lyerxa.htm>

Ed Young is the illustrator of *The Turkey Girl* and other picture books. He was born in China and attended college in the United States.
<www.edupaperback.org/authorbios/Young_Ed.html>

Youyouseyah, **Getting Ready** (Hopi, Tewa) is a coauthor of *When Hopi Children Were Bad*. Like his sister, Tawa Mana, he loves the traditions of his people.

Appendix A

Publishers

Abbeville Press
116 W. 23rd Street, Suite 500,
New York, NY 10011
Telephone 646-375-2039 Fax 646-375-2040
<www.abbeville.com/>

Abingdon Press
201 Eighth Avenue South, P.O. Box 801,
Nashville, TN 37202-0801
Telephone 800-251-3320 Fax 800-836-7802
<www.abingdon.org/>

American Historical Association
400 A Street, SE, Washington, DC 20003-3889
Telephone 202-544-2422 Fax 202-544-8307
<www.theaha.org>

Anoai Press
3349-A Anoai Place, Honolulu, HI 96822
Telephone 808-988-6109 Fax 808-988-1119
<www.anoaipress.com>

Beyond Words Publishing
20827 N.W. Cornell Road, Suite 500,
Hillsboro, OR 97124-9808
Telephone 503-531-8700 Fax 503-531-8773
<www.beyondword.com>

Bishop Museum Press
1525 Bernice Street, Honolulu, HI 96817-2704
Telephone 808-848-4159 Fax 808-847-8249
<www.bishopmuseum.org/press/>

Book Publishing Company
P.O. Box 99, Summertown, TN 38483
Telephone 888-260-8458
<www.bookpubco.com/home.html>

Bridgestone Books/Capstone Press
151 Good Counsel Drive, P.O. Box 669,
Mankato MN 56002-0669
Telephone 800-747-4992 Fax 888-262-0705
<www.Capstone-Press.com>

BridgeWater Books, *See* **Troll**

Charlesbridge Publishing
85 Main Street, Watertown, MA 02472
Telephone 617-926-0329 or 800-225-3214
Fax 617-926-5720
<www.charlesbridge.com>

Chelsea House
65250 Baltimore Pike, Yeadon, PA 19050
Telephone 800-362-9786 Fax 610-359-1439
<www.chelseahouse.com>

Children's Book Press
2211 Mission Street, San Francisco, CA 94110
Telephone 415-821-3080 Fax 415-821-3081
<www.cbookpress.org>

Chronicle Books
85 Second Street, 6th Floor,
San Francisco, CA 94105
Telephone 415-537-4256 Fax 415-537-4420
<www.chroniclebooks.com>

Clarion Books, *See* **Houghton Mifflin**

Clear Light Publications
823 Don Diego, Santa Fe, NM 87501
Telephone 888-253-2747 Fax 505-989-9519
<www.clearlightbooks.com>

Cobblestone Publishing
30 Grove Street, Suite C,
Peterborough, NH 03458
Telephone 800-821-0115 or 603-924-7209
Fax 815-224-6615
<www.cobblestonepub.com>

Council Oak Books
1350 East 15th Tulsa, OK 74120
Telephone 918-587-6454 or 800-247-8850
Fax 918-583-4995

Dial Books for Young Readers/Penguin Putnam
375 Hudson Street, New York, NY 10014
Fax 212-414-3399
<www.penguinputnam.com>

DK Publishing
375 Hudson Street, New York, NY 10014
Telephone 212-213-4800 Fax 212-213-5240
<www.usstore.dk.com>

Dover Publications
11 East Second Street,
Mineola, NY 11501-3852
Fax 516-742-6953
<http://store.doverpublications.com/>

Dutton Children's Books, *See* **Penguin Putnam**

Econo-Clad Books
Sagebrush Corporation
Telephone 800-255-3502 Fax 800-628-2410
<www.sagebrushcorp.com/books/>

EMC Publishing
875 Montreal Way, St. Paul, MN 55102-4245
Telephone 800-328-1452 Fax 800-328-4564
<www.emcp.com/>

F. Watts, *See* **Grolier**

Fulcrum Publishing
16100 Table Mountain Parkway, Suite 300,
Golden, CO 80403-1672
Telephone 800-992-2908 or 303-277-1623
Fax 800-726-7112 or 303-279-7111
<www.fulcrum-books.com>

Graphic Arts Center Publishing/Alaska Northwest, WestWinds Press
3019 NW Yeon, Portland, OR 97210
Telephone 503-226-2402 Fax 503-223-1410
<www.gacpc.com/gacpc/index.asp>

Greenfield Review Press
2 Middle Grove Road,
Greenfield Center, NY 12833
Telephone 518-583-1440 Fax 518-583-9741
<www.greenfieldreview.org/>

Grolier
Telephone 800-621-1115 x 2660
<http://publishing.grolier.com/>

Groundwood Books
720 Bathurst Street, Suite 500,
Toronto, Ontario M5S 2R4
Telephone 416-537-2501 Fax 416-537-4647
<www.groundwoodbooks.com>

Hancock House
1431 Harrison Avenue, Blaine, WA 98230-5005
Telephone 604-538-1114 Fax 604-538-2262
<www.hancockhouse.com>

Harcourt
525 B Street, Suite 1900, San Diego, CA 92101
Telephone 619-699-6598
Fax 619-699-6777 or 800-221-2477
<www.harcourt.com>

HarperCollins
1350 Avenue of the Americas,
New York, NY 10019
Telephone 212-261-6500 Fax 800-822-4090
<www.harperchildrens.com>

Harry N. Abrams
100 Fifth Avenue, New York, NY 10011
Fax 212-929-4773
<www.abramsbooks.com/index2.html>

Heard Museum
2301 North Central Avenue,
Phoenix, AZ 85004-1323
Telephone 602-252-8344
<www.heard.org/>

Holiday House
<www.migdale.com/lmhhb.html>

Houghton Mifflin
215 Park Avenue South, New York, NY 10003
Telephone 212-420-5800 Fax 212-420-5850
<www.hmco.com>

Hyperion Books for Children
114 Fifth Avenue, New York, NY 10011
Telephone 212-633-4400
<disney.go.com/disneybooks/hyperionbooks/homepage.html>

Island Heritage
94-411 Ko'aki Street, Waipahu, HI 96797
Telephone 808-564-8800 or 800-468-2800
Fax 808-564-8877
<www.islandheritage.com>

Kids Can Press
4500 Witmer Estates,
Niagara Falls, NY 14305-1386
Fax 416-960-5437
<www.kidscanpress.com>

Kiva Publishing
21731 E. Buckskin Dr. Walnut, CA 91789
Telephone 800-634-5482 or 909-595-6833
Fax 909-860-5424
<www.kivapub.com>

Kivaki Press
21 Look Road, Arden, NC 28704-8401

Lee & Low Books
95 Madison Avenue, New York, NY 10016
Telephone 888-320-3395 or 212-779-4400
Fax 212-532-6035
<www.leeandlow.com>

Lerner Publishing
241 First Avenue North,
Minneapolis, MN 55401-1607
Telephone 612-332-3344 or 800-328-4929
Fax 612-332-7615
<www.lernerbooks.com>

Little, Brown and Company, Time Warner
1271 Avenue of the Americas,
New York, NY 10020
<www.twbookmark.com/>

Macmillan Books for Young Readers, *See* **Simon & Schuster**

Makoché Recording Company
208 N. 4th Street, P.O. Box 2756,
Bismarck, ND 58502-2756
Telephone 701-255-8284 or 800-637-6863,
701-223-7316
<www.makoche.com>

Minnesota Historical Society Press
345 Kellogg Blvd. W., St. Paul, MN 55102-1906
Telephone 651-297-3243 or 800-647-7827
Fax 651-297-1345
<www.mnhs.org/mhspress>

Modern Curriculum Press
4350 Equity Drive, P.O. 2649,
Columbus, Ohio 43216-2649
Fax 410-315-9630
<www.pearson.com>

Morrow Junior Books
1350 Avenue of the Americas,
New York, NY 10019
<www.simonides.org/books/publishers/wilmac.html>

Mutual Publishing
1215 Center Street, Suite 210, Honolulu, HI
Telephone 808-732-1709 Fax 808-734-4094
<www.mutualpublishing.com>

National Geographic Society
1145 17th Street NW,
Washington, DC 20036-4688
<www.nationalgeographic.com>

Native Discovery, Inc.
P.O. Box 62657, Colorado Springs, CO 80962
Telephone 719-282-7747 Fax 719-282-4113
<www.nativediscovery.com>

The New Press
450 W. 41st St., New York, NY 10036
Telephone 212-629-8811 Fax 212-629-8617
<www.thenewpress.com/>

Northland Publishing
P.O. Box 1389, Flagstaff, AZ 86002-1389
Telephone 800-346-3257 Fax 800-257-9082
<www.northlandpub.com>

Orchard Books, *See* **Grolier**

Oryx Press, *See* **Grolier**

Parabola
656 Broadway, New York, NY 10012
Telephone 212-505-6200 Fax 212-979-7325
<www.PARABOLA.org>

Penguin Putnam
375 Hudson Street, New York, NY 10014
Telephone 800-788-6262 Fax 212-366-2679
<www.penguinputnam.com/>

Perfection Learning
1000 North Second Avenue, P.O. Box 500,
Logan, IA 51546-0500
Telephone 800-831-4190 Fax 800-543-2745
<www.perfectionlearning.com/>

Philomel, *See* **Penguin Putnam**

PowerKids Press/Rosen Publishing Group
29 E. 21st Street, New York, NY 10010
<www.powerkidspress.com/>

R. C. Owen Publishers
P.O. Box 585, Katonah, NY 10536
Telephone 914-232-3903 Fax 914-232-3977
<www.rcowen.com/>

Raintree Steck Vaughn
15 East 26th Street, New York, NY 10010
Telephone 646-935-3702 Fax 646-935-3713
<www.steckvaughn.com>

Random House Children's Books
1540 Broadway, New York, NY 10036
Fax 212-940-7381
<www.randomhouse.com>

Rich-Heape Films
5952 Royal Lane, Suite 254-4,
Dallas, TX 75230
Telephone 888-600-2922 Fax 214-696-6306
<www.richheape.com>

Rising Moon/Northland Publishing
2900 N. Fort Valley Road, Flagstaff, AZ 86001
Telephone 928-774-5251 or 800-346-3257
Fax 800-257-9082
<www.northlandpub.com>

Runestone Press, *See* **Lerner Publishing**

Salina Bookshelf
1254 W. University Ave., Suite 130,
Flagstaff, AZ 86001
Telephone 877-527-0070 or 928-527-0070
Fax 928-526-0386
<www.salinabookshelf.com>

Scholastic
555 Broadway, New York, NY 10012-3999
Telephone 212-343-6100
<www.scholastic.com>

Scholastic Reading Counts
<src.scholastic.com/ecatalog/readingcounts/
index.htm>

Sierra Oaks Publishing Company
P.O. Box 255354, Sacramento, CA 95865-5354

Silver Whistle, *See* **Harcourt Brace**

Simon & Schuster
1230 Avenue of the Americas,
New York, NY 10020
Telephone 800-223-2336 Fax 212-698-4350
<www.simonandschuster.com>

Soundings of the Planet
P.O. Box 4472, Bellingham, WA 98227
Telephone 800-93-PEACE
<www.soundings.com>

Storytribe Publishing
4417 Morningside Way,
Canyon Lake, TX 78133
Telephone 830-899-5678
<www.docmoore.com/storytribe.html>

Syncopated Press
P.O. Box 411 Plainwell, MI 49080
Telephone 877-867-7737 Fax 616-685-6765

Troll Associates
100 Corporate Drive, Mahwah, NJ 07430
Telephone 800-929-8765 Fax 800-979-8765
<www.troll.com/>

Tundra Books
481 University Avenue, Suite 900,
Toronto, ON M5G 2E9
Telephone 416-598-4786 Fax 416-598-0247
<www.tundrabooks.com>

Two Canoes Press
P.O. Box 334, Hopkinton, MA 01748
Telephone 508-529-6034 Fax 508-529-6005
<www.twocanoespress.com/>

UglyTown
7336 Santa Monica Blvd. #683,
West Hollywood, CA 90046-6616
Telephone 213-484-8334 Fax 231-483-5620
<www.uglytown.com>

University of Arizona Press
355 S. Euclid Avenue, Suite 103,
Tucson, AZ 85719-6654
Telephone 520-621-1441 Fax 520-621-8899
<www.uapress.arizona.edu/home.htm>

University of Nebraska Press
233 North 8th Street, Lincoln, NE 68588-0255
Telephone 402-472-2298
Fax 800-526-2617 or 402-472-0308
<www.nebraskapress.unl.edu>

University of New Mexico Press
1720 Lomas Blvd. NE,
Albuquerque, NM 87131-1591
Telephone 505-277-7553 Fax 505-277-9270
<www.unmpress.com>

University of Oklahoma Press
4100 28th Ave. NW, Norman, OK 73069-8218
Telephone 405-325-2000 or
          800-627-7377 (orders only)
Fax 405-364-5798 or
          9800-735-0476 (orders only)
<www.oupress.com/>

Various Indian Peoples/(VIP) Publishing
P.O. Box 833216,
Richardson, TX 75083-3216
Telephone 800-776-0842 or 972-671-3525
Fax 972-671-3529
<www.nativelanguages.com>

Walker & Company
435 Hudson Street, New York, NY 10014
Telephone 212-727-8300 or 800-289-2553
Fax 212-727-0984 or 800-218-9367
<www.walkerbooks.com/>

WestWinds Press, *See* **Graphic Arts Center**

Wolfhouse Publishing
P.O. Box 1546, Woodinville, WA 98072
<http://home.earthlink.net/~wolfhouse/
          author.html>

Yellow Moon Press
P.O. Box 381316, Cambridge, MA 02238
Telephone 617-776-2230 Fax 617-776-8246
<www.yellowmoon.com>

Appendix B

Index

Collective names and tribal groups are indicated with a * before the terms.

Abbeville Press 9, 29, 30, 34, 103
*Abenaki 8, 12, 28, 35, 42, 46, 48, 60, 75, 87, 100
Abingdon Press 13, 25, 65, 103
*Acoma Pueblo 96
activist 92, 94
activity programs in education......................74
Adair, Mary...82
aged..63
Aguilar, Dugan 78, 85
Akweks, Kayeri 71, 85
ALA Best Books 25, 61, 66
ALA Notable Books 11, 15, 23, 45, 52
Alabama Emphasis on Reading (list)............22
Alaska.....................30, 34, 55, 76, 92, 102, 104
Alberta, Canada 64, 93, 94, 95
alcoholism 16
Alexie, Sherman..7
*Algonkian 42
*Algonquian 15
*Algonquin 15
Allen, Joe 64, 85
Allen, Paula Gunn 7, 57, 60, 85
alphabet..69-72
Amelia Frances Howard-Gibbon 53, 95
America-discovery 15, 19
American bison 23
American Historical Association 83, 103
American Indian Literature 55
American Indian Songs... 56

American literature 53
American poetry 34, 52, 54, 55
Andreasen, Dan 12, 85
animals..........8, 10, 30-31, 33, 36-37, 43-45, 82
*Anishinabe 32, 49, 67
Aniyunwiya 55
Anoai Press..53, 103
Antelope Woman 93
An Anthology of Alaskan... 56
An Anthology of... 55-56
antiquities...55, 60
*Apache 31-32, 48-50, 63-64, 68-70, 91, 100-101

Apache Children and Elders... 68
The Apaches 63
Apes, William 59
*Arapaho 32
*Arawak 19
Arcade (Press) 57
archaeology 60
Archuleta, Margaret...59
Arizona 9, 36, 57, 76, 86-88, 91-93, 95-99, 101-102, 107
Arkansas Diamond (list) 16
Arkeketa, Annette...41
Armitage, Kimo 17-19, 79, 85
Armstrong, Jeannette 7
Arneach, Lloyd..48
Arnett, Carroll 51
Arrow Lakes Region 74, 94
The Arrow over the Door 8
art 53, 59, 74, 82-83, 85-86, 88-89, 91-92, 96-97, 100-101
artisan...62
artists 81
Aruego, Jose 34, 86
As Long as the Rivers Flow 60

Appendix B: Index   *109*

Asato, Dennis 53, 86
Ashkii's Journey 8
*Assiniboine..49, 87
Ata, Te 28, 86, 95
Attla, Catherine 27
Au, Joy S. 34, 86
Audio Bookshelf..8
Audiofile..45-46
Audiofile Editor's (Award) 45
August House 56
Aunt Lute Books 57
auroras 23
authorship 75
Autumn Morning Star 48
Avon 55, 68
Awiakta, Marilou 51, 59
Azarian, Mary 54, 86
Azhé'é bikénidoots'osii 13

babies 53
Baby Rattlesnake 28, 95, 97
Bacchin, Giorgio 62, 86
Bachofner, Carol 51
Badger Woman 48
Baker, Marie Annharte 51
Ballard, Charles 51
ballerinas 70
ballet dancers 70
Bamboo Ridge Press 56
Barnes, Jim 51
Barreiro, José 7
Basile, Dorothea..83
baskets 62, 79
Battle of the Books (list) 21
Battlefields and Burial... ....60, 89
Baviera, Rocco 61
BCCB 68
Beacon Press 57
Bears Make Rock Soup... ....8, 89
Bedford, Denton 7
Begay, Jason 41
Begay, Shonto 71-72, 86
Beginning Biographies series 70
Bell, Betty Louise..7
*Bella Coola 35
Benson, Diane 41, 51
Bernardin, James 33, 86
Best Bets (list) 20
Best Book (list) 19
Best Book of the Year (list).........................19
Between Earth & Sky 28
Beyond Words Pub. 14, 70-71, 103
Big Eagle 49

Big Mountain, Tucson 48
BigEagle, Duane 51
Bighorse, Tiana 59
Bigjim, Fred 41, 51
Bigtree, Danny 12
bilingual 13, 63, 79
biography 60-62, 66, 68, 70, 74-75, 77-78
The Birchbark House 8
Birchfield, D. L. 55, 59
Bird, Gloria 51, 56
birds 19, 33, 44
Bishop Museum Press 36, 103
bison 23, 38
Black Elk 78
Blackbird, Andrew J. 59
*Blackfoot 358, 50, 68-69
Blackfoot Children and Elders... 68
Blackhawk (Walters) 48
Blackhawk, Ned 76, 86
Blackstone, Tsianina Redfeather 41
Blackwell Anthologies series 56
Blackwell Publishers 56
Blaeser, Kimberly......................................51
Blanche, Jerry D. 56
Blevins, Win (Winfred) 7
blind 22
Blood, Charles L. 13, 86
Bloomfield, New Mexico 68
Bloomsbury Review 10, 28
Blowsnake, Sam 59
Blue Cloud, Peter 51
The Blue Roses 9, 87
Blue Wolf, James 51
Blumenschein, E. L. 66, 86
Bock, William Sauts Netam'xwe................40
Bones in the Basket 29
Book News, Inc. 77
Book Publishing Company 78, 103
The Book Report 31-32, 71
Bookbuilder's West Award........................31
Booklist 8-23, 28-35, 37-39, 46-47, 52-54,
                    60-62, 64-68, 72-74, 76-78
Borden, William..51
Bosque Redondo 8, 72
Bourdeau, Jan (Waboose)..........13, 19, 23, 101
Bowen, DuWayne Leslie 38, 87
Bowman's Store 60
A Boy Called Slow 61, 86
Boy Scouts 66, 89
Boyden, Linda 9, 87
Bragg, Lynn 74, 87, 94
A Braid of Lives 61
Braine, Susan..63, 87

Brandon, William 56
Brashear, Charles..7
Brave Wolf and the... ....29, 94-95
Bridgestone Books..73, 103
BridgeWater Books 31-32, 52, 70, 74, 103
Brigham, Besmilr..51
Bright Sun 94
British Columbia 74, 96, 95, 98
Brito, Silvester 51
Broker, Ignatia 72, 87
Brooklyn Museum 82-83
brothers 10, 13, 19, 30
brothers and sisters 10, 19
Browne, Vee 70, 87
Bruchac, James 34, 48, 71, 83, 87
Bruchac, Joseph......8, 10-12, 15, 17, 21-23, 28,
   31-34, 39-40, 43, 45-48, 52, 54-57, 60-61,
   68-69, 71-72, 74-75, 77, 82, 85, 87, 93
Bruchac, Marge 48
Bryan, Nonabah G. 83
Buckley, Ray..13, 25, 65, 87
buffalo...83
Bullchild, Percy 27
Bulletin of the Center... ....21, 36
Burns, Diane 51
Burrus, S. S. 32, 87
Bush, Barney 51
The Butterfly Dance 9, 88

*Caddo 32, 49
Caduto, Michael J. 82
Cajete, Gregory A. 82
Caldwell, E. K. (Kim) 59
California 9, 15, 19-20, 25, 31, 66, 78-79,
   83, 85-86, 90, 92-93, 97-99, 102
California Department of Education 9, 15, 20,
   25
Callahan, S. Alice..7
Camp Fire Girls 67, 89
Campbell, Maria 73, 88
Canada............13, 20, 23-24, 48, 64, 73, 77, 88,
   90, 93-94, 99-101
Canadian...Children's Librarians 53
Canyon, Christopher 11, 88
Capitol Choices (list) 22
Cardiff, Gladys 51
Carr, A. A. (Aaron Albert) 7
cats 14
Ceremony-in the Circle of Life 10
Champagne, Duane 59
Charlesbridge Publishing 67, 103
Charlie May Simon (list) 16
Charlotte Zolotow Award 14

Chelsea House 69, 103
*Cherokee ..16-17, 28, 31-35, 39, 41-42, 44, 46,
   48, 50, 54-55, 63-64, 77, 87-88, 91-93, 95-100
Cherokee Children's Songs 42
Cherokee Scary Stories 42
The Cherokees 63
*Cheyenne 28, 32, 35, 37, 46, 64, 78, 87
The Cheyennes 63
*Chickasaw 28
Chief Lelooska 39, 93
Child, Brenda 59
Children of Clay 61
Children of the Longhouse 10
children's art..74
Children's Book Council 62
Children's Book Press 8, 19, 24, 28, 73, 77, 103
Children's Bookwatch 77
children's plays..46
children's poetry 34, 52-55
children's writings 53, 55
*Chipewyan 64, 95
chipmunks 34, 45
*Chippewa 37, 49
*Choctaw 18, 42, 48
The Choctaw Way 42
Choice 36, 54
Christmas 10, 13, 65-66, 97
Chronicle Books 30, 73, 103
Chrystos 51
*Chuckchee 29
Churchill, Ward 59
Cinderella 39
The Circle of Thanks 52
Circle of Wonder 10
CIRI Foundation 55
Clambake 62
clambakes...62
Clarion Books 61, 66, 104
Clark, Beth 38, 88
Clark, William 21
Clarke, Peter Dooyentate.....................................59
Clear Light Publications 10, 38, 104
Clements, Marie..41
Clements, Susan..51
Clinton, Verna 8, 88
Cloudwalker 11
Coates, Ross....................................32, 40, 65, 88
Cobblestone Publishing......................82, 104
Coffee House Press 57
Coffin, Tom 30, 88
Cogewea, the Half Blood....................................7
Coke, Allison (Adelle) Hedge.........................51
coloring books 79

Columbus, Christopher	29, 71
*Comanche	37, 49
Comfort, Carol	57
coming of age	8, 68
conduct of life	18, 77
Conley, Robert J.	7, 27
Contemporary American...	56-57
Contemporary Native...	55-57
Contemporary Poetry and...	57
Contemporary Poetry by...	57
Cook-Lynn, Elizabeth	7
Cooperative Children's...	14, 20, 65
Copway, George	59
Córdova, Amy	9, 88
corn	35, 45, 64, 85, 91
Cornplanter	87
costume	75
Council for Indian Education	81
Council Oak Books	15, 25, 104
Cover-to-Cover Books	14, 18
coyote	29-31, 42-44, 46, 88, 95
Coyote and Rock	42
Coyote Columbus	29, 95
Coyote in Love with a Star	30, 88
Coyote Sings to the Moon	30
Crazy Horse	11
Crazy Horse's Vision	11
creation	13, 29, 34, 36, 42, 45-46, 73
Creation Story	42
*Cree	29, 49, 54, 64, 77, 90, 95
Cree, Francis	43, 88
*Creek	16, 17, 33, 48, 88, 91, 98
Cross, Donna	48
Cross, Joe	48
Crow Hiendlmayr, Jackalene	48
*Crow	29, 69, 95
Crow Children and Elders...	69
Crow Dog, Leonard	59
Crow Dog, Mary	59
culture	30, 69, 71-72, 74-76, 78-79, 83, 87, 93, 96, 98, 102
Curse of the Royal Ruby	22
Cusick, David	59
*Dakota	16, 25, 49, 61, 64-65
*Dakota Sioux	89
Dallas Morning News	9, 30
dams	74
dance	9, 17, 23, 34, 39, 55, 68, 75, 88, 97
Dancing Teepees	52
Dat-so-la-lee	62
Dat-so-la-lee: Artisan	62
Dawavendewa, Gerald	9, 88
Day with a Pueblo	62, 96
De Coteau Orie, Sandra	11, 88
De Montaño, Martha Kreipe	30, 88
Decade's Best Multicultural (list)	21
A Dear America Book	17
death	9, 14, 20-21, 98
DeClue, Charlotte	51
Deines, Brian	23, 89
Dekalb County (list)	25
Dell	57
Deloria, Ella Cara	7, 59
Deloria, Vine, Jr.	83
Denali Press	56
Des os Dans un Panier	29
Deux Plumes Et La Solitude...	35
Devilfish Bay	30
Dewey, Ariane	34, 86
Dial, Adolph L.	69, 89
Dial Books	8, 10, 12, 15, 18, 31, 33-35, 104
diaries	17
Did You Hear Wind...	11, 88
*Diné	32, 71, 87
disabilities	15
discoveries in geography	29
Diversity within America series	83
DK Publishing	39, 104
Dog People	12
*Dogrib	100
dogs	12
Doner, Kim	15, 25, 89
Dorris, Michael	15, 19, 22, 25, 89
Dorothy Canfield Fisher (award)	9
Doubleday	55, 57
Dover Publications	56, 66, 83, 104
Downing, Todd	7
Dream Feather	12, 96
Dreams and Thunder	55
Drumbeat...Heartbeat	63
Dunn, Ann M.	27
Dunn, Carolyn	57
Dunn, Matthew	64
Durable Breath	55
Dutton	68, 104
Eagle Heart	88
Eagle Song	12, 85
eagles	15
Earling, Debra Magpie	7
Earth Power Coming	55
Earth Song, Sky Spirit	55
Earth Maker's Lodge	82
The Earth Under...	52
East (U.S.)	34

Eastman, Charles A. 27, 66, 78, 86, 89
Echo-Hawk, Bunky, Jr. 41
Echo-Hawk, Roger C. 60, 89
Echo-Hawk, Walter R. 89
Echoes of the Night 42
ecology 59, 65-66
Econo-Clad............10, 12, 15, 19-22, 28, 31-32,
            35-36, 38, 52, 56-57, 65, 72-73, 77, 104
Eddy, Paul 49
Edmonds, Dayton 49
education 74
Egawa, Keith 7
The Elders Speak 43
Elementary School Library (list) 28, 52
EMC Publishing......................................16, 104
The EMC Masterpiece 16
Emerson, Anthony Chee 54, 89
Encyclopedia of the First... 82
Endrezze (Danielson), Anita 51
Enduring Wisdom...................................63, 98
English language 70
Enos, Solomon..79, 89
environmental aspects 74
Erdrich, Heid E. 51, 57
Erdrich, Lise 8, 89
Erdrich, Louise 8, 89
Et Le Cheval Nous a Ete Donne.....................35
ethnic identity 71
Evans, Ron...44, 49, 90
Ewing, Carolyn 38, 90
explorers 29, 78
Eyen, Jennifer Pierce......................................51

F. Watts...104
fabrics..14, 76
Fadden, David Kanietakeron 37, 82, 90
Fadden, John Kahionhes 37, 82-83, 90
Fadden, Ray Tehanetorens 43, 78, 99
fairs...54, 93
family 9, 18, 20, 24-25, 53, 61, 70, 73-74, 76,
                         86-87, 89-90, 92-97, 99-100
Father's Boots 13
Fernandez, Melanie 82
festivals..67, 69, 100
Fifield, Lisa 8, 90
Fifty Multicultural Books (list)................14, 20
fire 30-31, 33, 35, 42, 44, 46
Fire Race 30, 93-94
Firedancers 13
Fireside Tales..43
First Americans Book series..........................63
First Peoples series 70
The First Strawberries 31, 101

fishes..18
Five Owls 73
Flavin, Teresa 46, 90
Florida 13, 69, 93, 97, 102
Florida Sunshine (award) 13, 22
The Flute Player 31, 93
Flying with the Eagle... 31
folklore 24, 27-41, 47, 52-54, 64, 71, 76,
                                              82, 98, 102
food 54, 59, 64, 67, 71
Forbes, Jack 7
Fort Chipewyan Homecoming 64
Fortunate Eagle, Adam 59
Four Seasons of Corn.........................64, 85, 91
Francis, Lee 83
Francisco, Nia 51
Frank, Della 51
friends 12, 17-19, 24, 92
frontier and pioneer life 18
Fulcrum 11-12, 37, 71, 82-83, 87, 104
funeral customs and rites 60

games 59, 71, 78, 82
Gamma State Author's Award......................15
Gammell, Stephen 82, 90
Gansworth, Eric ....iv, 7
Garcez, Antonio 7, 27
gardening 9, 82
Geiogamah, Hanay 41
genealogy 59, 76-77
George, Dan 51
Georgia Children's Book Award 9
Getting Ready 102
The Ghost and Lone Warrior 32
ghost stories 38
Giese, Paula 81
Gift Horse 65
The Gift of the Great Spirit.........................43
Ginn 20
Giornata con un indiano Taos 62
The Girl Who Married the Moon 32, 87
girls...20
Gish, Robert Franklin 7
The Give-Away 13
Giving Thanks 65, 97
Gladstone, Jack 49
Glancy, Diane................................7, 41, 57
Gluskabe Stories 43
The Goat in the Rug 13, 86, 93, 96
God's Love Is Like 65
Goetzl, Robert F. 70, 74, 90
Goingback, Owl 7
golden eagle 15

Appendix B: Index *113*

Golden Sower (Award) 15
Gomez, Terry 41
Gonzales, Rosemary 82
Gonzalez, Bobby 49
The Good Luck Cat..14
Good Mind Records......................................45
Gordon, Roxy 51
Gorman, R. C. 57
Gottfriedson, Garry 51
Gould, Janice 51
Gourd Woman 43, 102
Grand Coulee Dam 74
grandfather..............9-10, 12, 15-16, 18, 20, 24,
 32-33, 40, 43-44, 62, 64, 88, 97
Grandfather Sings-Alone's... 44
Grandfather's Stories 44
Grandfather's Story of... ....32, 88, 97
Grandma Spider Brings the Fire 44
Grandmother Spider... ....33, 86, 92
Grandmother's Christmas Story 65, 97
grandmothers.......................................13, 17
grandparents 15, 85, 89
Graphic Arts Center...........................104, 107
gratitude 52
Graves, Sharol 73, 90
The Great Ball Game 33, 97
The Great Change 14, 90
Great Eagle and Small One 14, 95
Great Lakes Region 30
Great Plains 8, 11, 64-65, 69, 73
The Great Spirit Horse 33
Great Stone Face (list)................................22
Green, Rayna 82
Green Bay Public Schools (list) 19
Green Grow the Lilacs 41
Green Snake Ceremony................................15
Greenfield Review Press 38, 55-57, 83, 87, 104
Greenwood Professional... 82
Greyfeather series 15, 25
grief..21
Grieves, Catron 51
Grigg, Carol 14, 90
Grolier 104, 106
Groundwood 17, 20, 29, 53, 82, 104
Growing Up Native American 55
Growing Up Native in Alaska 55
Guerrier Solitaire et le... 32
Guests 15
A Guide to Evaluating... 82

H. W. Wilson's... ....19, 22, 28, 52
Hail, Raven 51
Haldane, Suzanne 68, 90

Hale, Chaika Piilani...............................53, 90
Hale, Janet Campbell 7, 59
Hale, Lilia Wahinemaika'i......................79, 90
Halfmoon, Ray 16
Hall, Dana Naone 56
Hamilton, Irene Nakai 74, 91
Hancock House 74, 104
hand weaving 14
handicapped..22
Haozous 91
Harcourt 14, 21, 23, 28, 47, 104, 106
Harjo, Barbara 59
Harjo, Joy..14, 56, 91
Harjo, Lisa D. 82, 83
Harper 56
Harper & Row 56
HarperCollins.....................16, 20, 22, 104
Harper's Anthology of 20th... 56
Harrell, Beatrice O. 18, 91
Harrington, John 70, 91
Harris, Ladonna 59
Harry N. Abrams 65, 104
harvest festivals...67
Harvest Moon..49
Harvey, Karen D. 82, 83
Hawai'i Sings 34, 100
Hawaii 18-19, 34, 53, 79, 87, 89-90
Hawaiian 18-19, 34, 53, 79, 87, 89-90
Hawaiian culture 79
healing 25, 45
Heard Museum 105
Heart, Mind, Body, Soul 56
The Heart of a Chief 15
Hello Reader series....................................38
Henry, George 59
Henry, Gordon 51
Henry, Roy 51
Hernández-Avila, Inés 51
*Hidatsa 102
High Elk's Treasure 16
Higheagle, Anthony 41
Highway, Tomson 41
Hilbert, Vi..42, 91
Hill, Roberta..51
Himler, Ronald....................................63, 91
Hirajeta, Onehawk.....................................49
Hirschfelder, Arlene B. 53
history............7-8, 17, 25, 29, 59, 64, 66, 68-78,
 83, 85-86, 89, 93-94
History of Joaquin Murieta 7
Hitakonanu'laxk..27
Hobson, Geary 7, 56
Hogan, Linda 7

Holiday House 16, 24, 52, 63, 105
Honolulu Star-Bulletin 53
Honolulu Weekly..53
hoop dance 68
Hooser, Phillip 41
*Hopewell..28
*Hopi 9, 28, 36, 42, 64, 88, 93, 99, 102
The Hopis 63
Hopkins, Sarah Winnemucca 59
Horn, Gabriel 102
Horn Book 9-12, 14-16, 18-20, 22-25, 29-33, 35, 37-39, 47, 53-55, 60-68, 70, 72-74, 76-78
Horn Book Fanfare 9, 19, 25
Horse Capture, George 59
horses 24, 33, 45, 65, 78, 100
Houghton Mifflin.................................104, 105
Houser, Allan C. 21, 91
How Chipmunk Got His Stripes 34, 86
How Rabbit Tricked Otter... 44
How Raven Stole the Sun 34, 102
How They Lived in Canada series 73
How to Teach about American... 82
How to Tell the Difference 82
How Turtle's Back Was Cracked 34, 44
How Two-Feather Was Saved 35
How We Saw the World 35
Howard, Gregg 42, 44, 47, 49, 91
Howe, LeAnne 7
Howell, Frank 47, 91
Hu, Ying-Hwa 16, 100
Hucko, Bruce 73, 91
human ecology..65, 66
human remains 60
hummingbirds 36
*Hunkpapa 68
Hunter, Nora 51
Hunter, Sally M..64, 91
Hyperion......................8-9, 15, 19, 22, 25, 105

Igniting the Sparkle 82
In a Sacred Manner I Live 66
Indian authors 53, 55, 61, 75
Indian ballerinas 70
Indian baskets 62
Indian Boyhood 66, 86
Indian children 11, 61, 71, 89
Indian dance 9, 17, 75
Indian mythology......................................35, 37
Indian Nations series...............................75, 76
Indian philosophy 61, 63, 66
Indian poetry 52, 57
Indian reservations 16
Indian Scout Craft and Lore 66

Indian Shoes..16, 94
Indian textile fabrics 14
Indian women 32, 60
Indian youth 52-53, 92
Indiana Read-Aloud (list) 22
Indiana University Press 57
Indians of Mexico 79
Indians of North America series 69
Ininatig's Gift of Sugar 67
Inktomi and the Ducks... 44
Institute of American...............95, 97, 101
intergenerational relations 69
International Reading Assn. ..11, 61-62, 68, 70
Into the Moon 56
*Inupiaq 32
Iowa Children's Choice (Award) 16
The Iroquois 63
*Iroquois................32, 43-45, 56, 64, 78
Iroquois Stories 45
Island Heritage 17-19, 79, 105
islands..9
Itse Selu 67, 96

Jackson, Jane K..83
Jacob, Murv 12, 34, 52, 92
Jacobs, Alex 51
James, Diana 30
James, Embert F. 30
James, George Suckinaw, Jr. 30
James, Rudy...30, 49, 92
Jane Addams (Award) 16
Jesus Christ 65
Jim, Rex 5
Jingle Dancer 16, 100
Joagquisho 94
Joe, Rita 51
Joe, Roberta 51
Johnson, Basil 27, 59
Johnson, E. (Emily) Pauline 51, 59
Johnson, Elias 59
Johnson, Janet 51
Johnson, Rodney 22, 92
Jones, Matthew 41, 49
Jones, Peter 59
The Journal of Jesse Smoke 17
journeys 22, 29
Junaluska, Arthur 41
Jumper, Betty Mae....................................27, 59
Jumper, Moses 51

Kabotie, Michael (Mike) 51
Kahionhes-Fadden, John 37, 82-83, 90
Kahkewaquonaby 59

Kakaygeesick, Robert, Jr. 23
Kake, Alaska...76
Kakkak, Dale 37, 92
Kaneshiro, Scott 17-19, 92
Kansas 9, 15, 88, 99
*Karok 31
Katz, Jane B. 78
Kauffman, John 41
Kavasch, E. Barrie 69, 75-76, 82, 92
Kavena, Juanita Tiger 59
Kayenta, Arizona 76, 86
Keams, Geri (Geraldine).............33, 46, 49, 92
Keepers of Life 82, 90
Keepers of the Animals 82
Keepers of the Earth 82
Keepers of the Night 82
Keeshig-Tobias, Lenore 56
Kenny, Maurice 51, 57
Keon, Wayne 51
kidnapping 22
Kids Can Press 20, 23, 105
Kilcup, Karen..56
Kimball, Yeffe..59
King, Sandra 75, 92
King, Thomas 29-30, 92
kings and rulers 60
kings, queens, rulers 61
Kinaaldá 67
Kinaaldá 67, 68
*Kiowa 35, 49-50, 95, 99-100
Kirk, Connie Ann 70, 92
Kirkus 8-12, 15-25, 28-29, 31, 33, 35-36,
        39, 52-54, 60-61, 64, 66, 68, 72, 77
Kiva Publishing 36, 54, 105
Kivaki Press 82, 105
Kneubuhl, Victoria 41
*Kootenai 94
Kottke, Theodore 41
Kraus, D. Bambi 76, 93
Kreipe de Montano, Martha 30, 88
Kuloscap & The Ghosts 42
Kumulipo 36
*Kwakiutl 83, 93

La Flesche, Francis 59
Lacapa, Michael................................31, 36, 93
LaDuke, Winona 7, 57
*Laguna Pueblo 85
Lake Superior Region 9
*Lakota 11, 22, 32, 47, 50, 65, 68-69, 90, 93,
                                                                    100
Lakota Hoop Dancer 68, 90, 93
Lakota Sioux Children... 69

The Lame Warrior and... 32
Lamplighter Award 21
Lang, Julian 31
Langley, Bertney 49
Last Leaf First Snowflake to Fall 53
Lasting Echoes 68
law and legislation.......................................60
Le Beau, Owen...41
Lee, Paul..14, 93
Lee & Low Books 9, 11, 60, 65, 105
Left Hand Bull, Jacqueline 68, 93
legal status, laws, etc. 60
Légendes Amérindiennes Sur... 29
legends 27-31, 35-38, 42, 54, 82
Leggitt, Marjorie C. 82
Lerner 60-64, 67, 70, 75-76, 78, 105-106
Lesley, Craig 57
Less Than Half, More Than Whole 93
lesson plans 81
Lessons from Mother Earth 17, 94
Lessons from the Animal People 45
Levasseur, Jo 82
Lewis and Clark Expedition 21, 74
Library Journal.......................................20, 75
Library of Intergenerational... 68
Library Talk..31, 32
The Lightning Within 56
Limu The Blue Turtle 17
Link, Martin..13, 93
Linklater, Eric 41
Little, Brown 39, 54, 66, 105
Little Fish..18, 94-95
Little Rainbow Books series 17-19
Little Thunder, Julie Pearson 59
Little Water and the... ....36, 78, 83, 93
Little Wolf, Linda...............................33, 78, 93
Littlebird, Harold..51
Littlechild, George.....................19, 24, 77, 93
Locke, Kevin 49, 68
Locker, Thomas 28, 52, 54, 93
Lomatuway'ma, Michael......................36, 93
Lomawaima, K. Tsianina 59
London, Jonathan 30, 54, 93
Long, Sylvia 30, 94
Longwalker..18
Longwalker's Journey 18, 91, 95
Louis, Adrian 7
Loyie, Larry 7
Lucero, Evelina 51
luck 14
*Lumbee...69, 87, 89
The Lumbee 69, 89
Lyons, Oren 16, 24, 94

Macmillan Books 72, 105
Madama, John 62, 94
Madsen, Jim..16, 94
The Magic Hummingbird 36, 93
The Magic World 56
Magnuson, Diane....................................77, 94
Mahalo e Grandpa 18
Maheo 42
*Maidu 85, 88
Maine Children's Book (list) 9
Maine Student Book (list) 22, 25
Makoché Recording....................43, 45, 105
Malama, Hawaiian Land... 56
*Malecite 37
Malotki, Ekkhart 36
Mama is Hapai 53
A Man Called Raven 19, 100
*Mandan 29
Mankiller, Wilma 59
Manuel, Vera 41
Manuli'i & the Colorful Cape 19
Many Circles, Many Paths 83
Many Nations 69, 90
Manyarrows, Victoria 51
maple 43, 67
Marchand, Virgil "Smoker"....................74, 94
Maria Tallchief, Prima Ballerina 70
Marks, Dea 18, 94
Marshall, Joseph III 7, 27
Martin, Linda R. 29, 94
Martinson, David 51
Maryland 12, 70, 101
Maryland Black-Eyed Susan (list) 22
Maryland Children's Book Award 12
Mashpee 62, 96
Massachusetts 15, 23, 62, 87, 94, 96, 101
Mathews, John Joseph 7, 59
Maui 36, 100
Maui, the Mischief Maker 36, 100
Maungwudaus 59
McAdams, Janet..51
McClanahan, A. J. 55
McDaniel, Wilma 51
McDonald, Anne 83
McDonald, Jerry Thundercloud 49
McGlashan, June 51
McKelvey, Celina 68
McLaughlin, Marie 27
McLeod, Elaine 17, 94
McLeod, John..41
McNally, Darren 64, 94
McNickle, D'Arcy 7, 21, 94
Means, Russell 59

Medawar, Mardi Oakley 7
medicine..45, 71, 95
Medicine Crow, Joe 29, 95
Medicine Path 45
Medicine Story..49
Meers, Tony 18, 95
Meet Naiche 70, 91
Meet the Author (series) 75
Mendoza, Vincent 59
*Menominee..92
Mercredi, Morningstar 64, 95
*Mescalero Apache 49
The Messenger of Spring 36
Messer, Randy 14, 95
Métis 19, 24, 64, 88, 95-96
Mexico 79
*Micmac..35, 37, 93, 98
Midge, Tiffany 51
Midwest Book Review 15, 77
Miguel, Gloria 41
Mihesuah, Devon 59
Milky Way 39, 99
Mills, Earl..59
Minnesota ..5, 7, 67, 72, 75, 87, 90-92, 96, 101, 105
Minnesota Historical Society 57, 72, 105
Miranda, Deborah 51
*Missouria 49, 101
Mitten, Lisa 81
mixed descent 60
Modern Curriculum Press................62, 70, 105
*Modoc..29, 89
*Mohawk 10, 12, 22, 29, 35, 37, 48-49,
                                  65, 70, 85, 90, 95, 99
The Mohawks of North America 70
Moisa, Ralph, Jr. 14, 18, 95
Mojica, Monique 41
Momaday, N. Scott 10, 95
Momaday, Natachee Scott 20, 95-96
Monkman, William Kent..........................29, 95
*Mono..79
Mono baskets 79
The Monster from the Swamp 37
monsters 32-33, 37, 40, 97
Montana................................29, 69, 87, 90, 94
months 54, 74
Monture, Joel................................7, 11, 95
moon 30, 32, 45, 54, 56, 87-87
Moore, Ramona 49
moral and ethical aspects 60
Morin, Paul 68, 95
Morning Girl..19
Morning on the Lake 19

Appendix B: Index **117**

Moroney, Lynn	28, 49, 95
Morrow	16, 55-56, 105
Mosely, Denise	41
Moses, Johnny	46, 49, 95
Mosionier, Beatrice Culleton	7, 23, 96
mother and child	53
Mourning Dove	7, 27, 59
The Mouse Couple	93
moving, household	12
Mr. Christie's Book (Award)	53
Multicultural Review	37, 52, 73, 95
*Muscogee Creek	16, 98
music	34, 45, 73
mutism	10
Mutual Publishing	34, 105
My Brother, The Bear	42
My Name Is America series	17
My Name Is Seepeetza	20
My Relatives Say	45
My World series	70
mystery and detective stories	22
mythology	29, 33, 35-37, 85
Na 'Olelo No'eau No Na Keiki	79
NAMMY Award	43, 44
Naranjo, Tito E.	62, 96
Nasdijj	59
Nasnaga	7
National Book Award	9, 89
National Council...Studies	52, 54-55, 61-62, 83
National Geographic Society	2, 105
National Museum...Indian	55, 88, 99
National Parenting (Award)	47, 82
Native American Animal Stories	37
The Native American Book of...	71
Native American Games...	71
Native American Gardening...	82
Native American Indian Resources	81
Native American Literature	55, 56
The Native American Look Book	82
Native American Reader	56
Native American Songs...	56
Native American Stories	37, 82, 90
Native American Wisdom	66
Native American Women...	56, 57
Native American Women's...	56, 57
Native Discovery	77, 105
native Hawaiian	85, 89, 90
Native People, Native Ways	71
Native Peoples Magazine	47, 94
Native Peoples series	73
Native Plant Stories	37, 90
Native Stories of the Origin of People	29
Native Voices series	57
The Native Women's Writing...	56
Native Writings after the Detours...	57
nature	10-11, 17, 37, 52-53, 59, 65, 78
*Navajo	8, 13-14, 20, 24, 28, 32-33, 46, 49, 54-55, 63-64, 67-68, 71-74, 76, 83, 86-89, 91-92, 94-95, 97-99, 102
Navajo ABC	71, 98
Navajo children	74
Navajo Community College Press	55
Navajo Native Dyes	83
Navajo language	13, 72
Navajo Long Walk	72
Navajo mythology	33
Navajo textile fabrics	14, 76
The Navajos	63
NCSA Crown Award	10
NCSS	9, 11, 28, 67
Nebraska	15, 20, 24, 56, 87, 107
Nelson, S. D.	11, 65, 96
Neon Pow-Wow	56
Nevada	62
New Hampshire	16
New Mexico	10, 21, 38-39, 54, 57, 61, 64, 68-70, 85, 88-89, 91, 95-99, 101-102, 107
New Native American Voices...	56
New Plymouth Colony	23
The New Press	105
New Voices Award	9
New Voices from the Longhouse	56
New York (state)	8, 22, 38, 86, 88
New York Times	9, 25
*Nez Percé	63, 64
The Nez Perce	63
Niatum, Duane	56
Nichols, Richard D.	76, 96
Night Flying Woman	72, 97
Nine Native Stories of...	35
Nolan, Yvette	41
*Nootka	49, 95
Normandin, Christine	39
North Carolina	89, 96, 99
North Dakota	22, 88-89, 102
Northeastern States	40, 101
*Northern Cheyenne	87
Northland Publishing	106
northSun, nila	51
Northwest Coast of North America	39
Northwest Territories	24
Notable...Global Society (list)	18
Notable Children's Books	9
Notable Children's Trade (list)	13, 17, 28, 62, 67

Notable Social Studies (list)	21, 24
Nowak, Mark	57
Oandasan, William	51
Occum, Samson	59
Octopus Lady and Crow	46
*Oglala	11, 38-39, 69
Ohio University Press	56
Ohiyesa	89
*Ohlone	102
*Ojibwa	9, 13, 20, 23, 36-37, 67, 72, 75, 78
*Ojibway	42-43, 46, 72, 75, 91-92, 98, 101
The Ojibway Dream	72
Oklahoma	11, 15, 17-18, 41, 55, 77, 86, 91-92, 95, 99, 100-101, 107
Oklahoma	41
Oklahoma Book Award	15
Oklahoma Library Association	11, 63
old age	13
Old Father Story Teller	38
Oliva, Judy Lee	41, 86
Oliver, Louis	51
One More Story	38
*Oneida	11-12, 35, 47
*Onondaga	94
Ontario, Canada	85, 89, 92-93, 95, 97-98, 101-102, 104
Ontario Library Assn.	20
Oraibi	36
oral tradition	41, 52, 68, 100
Orchard Books	53, 106
Ortiz, Alfonso	27
Ortiz, Simon J.	7, 55, 73, 96
Oryx American Family Tree	76
Oryx Press	76, 106
*Osage	29, 32, 50, 70
Oskison, John Milton	7, 59
*Otoe	49, 101
Otto, Simon	27
outdoor life	59, 67
Owens, Helen	41
Owens, Louis	7
Owens, Robert	41
Owl in the Cedar Tree	20, 96
Oyate	8-14, 17, 20-21, 23-25, 30-32, 34-35, 38, 54, 60, 65-67, 74, 81-83
Pacific Northwest Young…	9
Padilla, (Viento) Stan	12, 79, 96
painter	88-89, 92-93
paintings	8, 39, 77, 98
*Paiute	85
Palamino, Jess Waking Horse	49
Palmer, Gus	51
*Papago	28, 50
parables	65
Parabola	42, 44-46, 106
Parabola Storytime	42, 44, 46, 106
parent and child	25
Parenting Magazine (Award)	47
Parent's Choice (Award)	11, 44, 48
Parent's Guide to Children's (Award)	47
Parker, Nancy Winslow	13, 96
Paschen, Elise	51
*Pawnee	60, 73, 89, 101
The Pawnee Nation	73
Peltier, Leonard	59
Pemmican Publications	23
Penguin Putnam	104, 106
Penn, W. S.	7
*Pennacook	15, 16
Pennington, Daniel	67, 96
People of the Buffalo	73, 99-100
The People Shall Continue	73, 90
Perceval, Don	20, 96
Perea, Robert	7
Perfection Learning	14, 18, 106
Perry, Lynette	59
Peters, Russell M.	62, 96
Peters, Sandra	41
Peters, Steven	62
Petit Ruisseau et le Don…	36
Pheasant, Daniel	46, 96
Pheasant, Driver	49, 96
Phelps, George	41
Philadelphia School District (list)	21
Philip, Neil	61, 66
Philomel	52, 54, 61, 106
philosophy	59, 61, 63, 66, 79
philosophy of life	79
photography	21
physically handicapped	22
pilgrims	23
Pinola, Lanny	30, 97
*Piscataway	70, 99
plants	9, 17, 37, 45, 82, 102
plays	33, 46
Poetry and Prose from…	56
Pollock, Penny	39, 54, 97
Polynesian deity	36
*Pomo	83, 97
Poolaw, Lynda	41
Popejoy, Fred Running Bear	49
Posey, Alexander Lawrence	51, 59
*Potawatomi	30, 48, 88
potters	61, 62

pottery craft 61
Power, Susan 7
Power and Place 83
PowerKids Press 69, 106
*Powhatan 49, 91
powwows 63, 75
Prairie Pasque (list) 11
pregnancy 53
prejudices 12, 71
Premo, Steven 72, 97
Price, Anna 51
Printup, Erwin, Jr. 65, 97
psychopaths 23
puberty rites 68
Publishers Weekly 9-12, 19, 21-22, 25,
 28, 31-32, 34-35, 65, 72-73
*Pueblo 32, 38, 61-63, 85, 96, 98-99, 101
Pushing Up the Sky 46, 90
puzzles 78, 83

Qoyawama, Polingaysi 7
Quakers 8
Querry, Ron 7
questions and answers 24
Quill and Quire 29
*Quinault 49
Quintasket, Christine 59
quotations 63

R. C. Owen Publishers 75, 106
Rabbit's Wish for Snow 38, 90, 99
rabbits 38
Race with Buffalo... 56
racially mixed people 25
Rain Is Not My Indian Name 20
rain dances 9
A Rainbow at Night 73, 91
Rainer, Howard 51
Raintree Steck-Vaughn 75-76, 106
Ramirez, Alex 27
Rancourt, Gerald 27, 42, 100
Random House 77, 106
rattlesnakes 28
Raven Tells Stories 56
ravens 19
Razor, Peter 59
Reading Is Fundamental (list) 21
Reading Rainbow 14, 54, 65
The Reading Teacher 28
Real Human Beings 55
recipes 78, 82
Reclaiming the Vision 83
Reczuch, Karen 19, 97

Red Corn, Charles 7
Red Hawk 49
Red Hawk, Richard 32, 65, 97
Red Shirt, Delphine 59
Redhair, Darlene 13
Reese, Liz 41
Reinventing the Enemy's Language 56
Reisberg, Veg 28, 97
religion 10, 25, 41, 5-60, 71, 73
relocation 77
The Remembered Earth 56
Rendon, Marcie 41
Returning the Gift 56
Returning the Gift Conference 83
Revard, Carter 51
Reyes, Lawney L. 59
Rich-Heape Films 46, 106
Riddle, Pax 7
Ridge, John Rollin 7, 51
Riggs, (Rolla) Lynn 41, 51
Riley, Patricia 55
Rising Moon 31, 33, 106
Rising Voices 53
rites and ceremonies 15, 25, 32, 62-63, 67-68
A River Lost 74, 87, 94
Robertson, Sarah Ann 83
Roessel, Jaclyn 76
Roessel, Monty 67, 76, 97
Rose, Wendy 51
Rosen, Kenneth 57
Ross, Gayle 32, 34, 39, 44, 49, 62, 97
Roth, Susan L. 33, 97
Rothenberg, Jerome 57
Ruffo, Armand 41
rugs 14
Runestone Press 62, 106
Runner in the Sun 21, 91
Running Grunion 49
Russell, Samuel 8

*Sac, Fox 48
Sacajawea 21
Sacajawea, Translator and Guide 74, 91
Sacred Twins and Spider Woman 46
Salazar, Alan 50
Salina Bookshelf 8, 13, 24, 106
Salisbury, Ralph 7, 51
*Salish 20, 94
salmon 74
salmon fisheries 74
Salmon Run Press 55
San Francisco Chronicle 28
San Souci, Daniel 10, 97

Sanchez, Carol Lee	51
Sanders, William	7
Santa Clara Pueblo	38, 61, 96, 98-99, 101
*Santee	66
Sarris, Greg	7
Schick, Eleanor	71, 98
Scholastic	15, 17, 38, 60, 106
School Library Journal	9-12, 14, 16-17, 19, 21-23, 28, 30-32, 34-36, 52, 54, 60-63, 65-66, 68, 72, 75-76
schools	12, 87, 90, 96, 100, 102
sea life	18
sea turtles	18
Seale, Doris	82, 83
seasons	9, 53, 54, 64, 74, 85, 90-91
Seasons of the Circle	74, 90
The Secret of Dead...	22, 92, 100
Le Secret du Bison Blanc	38
The Secret of the White Buffalo	38
Seeing the Circle	75
Seeking a Guardian Spirit	45
Sees Behind Trees	22
*Seminole	16, 63-64, 69, 75
Seminole Children and Elders...	69
The Seminoles	63, 75
*Seneca	28, 36-38, 87-88, 92, 101-102
Sequoyah	11, 67
Sequoyah Children's Book list	11
Seven Native American Plays...	46
Seven Sisters	42
Shaking the Pumpkin	57
Shannon	75
Shaw, Anne Moore	59
Shaw, Fred	50
Shaw, Jerry	50
*Shawnee	15, 25, 50, 90, 101
Shed, Greg	23, 98
Shilling, Arthur	72, 98
Shining Way	42
Shiprock, New Mexico	54, 99
Short Fiction by Native...	57
Short Fiction in Native...	55
Short Stories of the...	55
Shorty, Robert	41
Shorty, Sharon	41
*Shoshone	21, 49, 76, 86
The Shoshone	76
*Shoshoni	74
Shropshire, Lola	41
Sickles, Dovie Thomason	43, 50, 100
Sierra Oaks Publishing	32, 40, 65, 106
*Siksiska	69
Silent Dreams	42
Silex, Edgar	51
Silko, Leslie Marmon	7, 51
Silvas, Abel	50
Silver Whistle	23, 68, 106
Silverman, Carolyn	83
Simon & Schuster	55, 105-106
Simpson, Michael	51
Singer, Beverly R.	53, 59
Sings-Alone, Duncan	44, 50, 98
*Sioux	25, 38-39, 54, 66, 69, 78, 85, 89, 92-93, 96, 98
The Sioux	63
Sister Nations	57
Sister Vision Press	56
sisters	10, 19, 23, 31, 42
Sit By My Fire	42
Sitting Bear	49
Sitting Bull	61
Six Nations Indian Museum	90, 99
Six Nations Singers	43
Skeleton Man	22
Skipping Stones Honor (Award)	23, 32
SkySisters	23, 89
Slapin, Beverly	82, 83
Slobod, Jeanne Lamar	83
Smelcer, John	51, 55
Smith, Cynthia Leitich	16, 20, 81, 94, 98
Smith, Don	93
Smith, Martin Cruz	7
Smith, Patricia Clark	51, 60, 98
Smith, R. T.	51
Sneve, Paul	63, 98
Sneve, Virginia Driving Hawk	16, 24, 52, 63, 98
*Snohomlish	46
social life and customs	18, 60-64, 66-67, 69, 71-74, 77-79
Society for...Tradition	44, 45
Society of Illustrators Award	31
solar eclipses	24
Songs from the Loom	76
Songs from This Earth...	57
Songs of Shiprock Fair	54
Songs of the Tewa	57
Soundings of the Planet	42, 106
Sounds True	45
South Dakota	11, 22, 68-69, 92, 98, 101
South Dakota Library Association	11
Southern states	17, 28, 33, 35, 67, 75, 77
Southwest	8, 13-14, 21, 24, 33, 38, 56, 63-64, 68
Southwest Children's Review	33
Sozap	87

Spain	23
Spanish	19, 28-29, 63, 65, 78
Speeches, addresses, etc.	65, 66
Spinden, Herbert Joseph	57
Spider Woman's Granddaughters	57
Spirit of the Cedar People	39
Spirit of the White Bison	23
Spotted Horse	96
spring	11-12, 36
Squanto	23
Squanto's Journey	23
Stands in Timber, John	59
stars	53
Steen, Bill	61, 98
Step into Reading series	77
stereotypes	12, 83
Sterling, Shirley	20, 98
Stewart, Don	67, 99
Stoddard Kids	13
Stories, Speeches, and Poems	56
Stories for a Winter's Night	57
Storm, Hyemeyohsts	7
The Story of the Inchworm	46
The Story of the Milky Way	39, 99
A Story to Tell	76
storytelling	13, 41, 47, 92, 100, 102
Storytribe Publishing	42, 44, 100, 106
strawberries	31, 47, 101
Stroud, Virginia A.	39, 99
student activities	83
A Student's Guide…Genealogy	76
sugar	67
sugar maple	67
Sullivan, Missy	82
sun	12, 24, 31, 33-34, 42, 47, 55, 86, 91-92, 94, 99, 100, 102
The Sun Dance Opera	55
Sun Girl	99
Sun Tracks series	57
Sundown	7
Sunpainters	24
Sunstone Press	57
The Surrounded	7
Swamp, Jake	65, 99
Swann, Brian	56
Sweet, Denise	51
Swentzell, Rina	61, 99
Syncopated Press	33, 78, 106
syrup	43, 67
Tafoya, Terry	50
*Taino	49
Tales of the People series	9, 29, 30
Tales of Wonder	47
Tales of Wonder II	47
Talking Leaves	57
Tallchief, Maria	70
TallMountain, Mary	51
*Taos	50, 62-63, 88
Taos aged	63
Taos Pueblo	63
Tapahonso, Luci	54, 71, 99
Tate, Douglas	73, 99
Tate, Joe	51
Tawa Mana	40, 99, 102
Tayac, Gabrielle	70, 99
Tayac, Naiche Woosah	70
Taylor, C. J.	13, 29, 32, 35-38, 99
Taylor, Drew Hayden	41
Tchin	38, 50, 99
Teaching about Native Americans	83
Teaching American Indian History	83
Teachers' Choice	11, 62, 70
teacher guides	81
Teaching Tolerance (magazine)	11
TeCube, Leroy	59
Tehanetorens, Ray Fadden	43, 78, 99
Tekaronianeken	99
Tell Me a Tale	47
Tennessee Volunteer State (list)	9
*Teton	22, 68
*Tewa	38, 57, 61-62, 93, 99, 101-102
Tewa Poetry	57
Tewa potters	62
Tewa pottery	62
Texas 2 by 2 (list)	17
Texas Bluebonnet (list)	22
Texas Lone Star (list)	22, 23
textile	14, 76
Thanksgiving	15, 23, 52
Thanksgiving: A Native Perspective	83
That's What She Said	57
Thirteen Moons on Turtle's Back	54, 93
This Land Is My Land	77, 93
ThlauGooYailthThlee	30, 92
Thomason, (Sickles) Dovie	43, 45, 48, 50, 100
Thompson, Earle	51
Thompson, Jill	22, 100
Thorndike Press	8, 9
Three Strands in the Braid	83
Through Indian Eyes	83
Through the Eye of the Deer	57
Thunderbird	29, 94-95
Timmons, Alice	41
Tingle, Tim	42, 44, 50, 100
The Tiny Warrior	77

Tipi Tales of the... 32
*Tlingit 30, 32, 34, 37, 46, 49, 76, 87, 92-93, 102
Tohe, Laura 51, 57
*Tohono O'Odham.................................35, 50
Tolentino, Doug Po'ola 34, 100
Toronto Star 29
Traditional Poetry of ... .57
Traditional Tales and... 57
Trafzer, Clifford E. 55
The Trail of Tears 77, 94
Trail of Tears 17, 42, 77
Trask, Haunani-Kay.......................................51
Tremblay, Gail 51
Tribe of Two Press 47, 83
Troll Associates 32, 74, 103, 107
trout 18
Trout, Lawana 56
Tsatsi 42, 100
Tsonakwa, Gerald Rancourt 27, 42, 100
Tucker, Wallace 41
*Tulalip..49
Tundra Books 29, 32, 35-38, 72, 107
Turcotte, Mark 51
The Turkey Girl 39, 102
turtles 18, 35
*Tuscarora 97
twins 10, 46
Two Canoes Press 44, 107
Two Leggings 78
Two-Rivers, E. Donald...................................41
Twofeathers, Shannon 73, 100
Tyler, D. D. 82
Tyrol, Adelaide Murphy................................82

UglyTown 22, 107
Underwood, Paula..................47, 83, 91, 100
University of Arizona............................88, 95, 99
University of Arizona Press.....................57, 107
University of California 56, 83
University of Chicago 93
University of Colorado 89
University of Nebraska Press 20, 24, 56, 107
University of New Mexico 89, 102,
University of New Mexico Press 10, 21, 57, 107
University of New York 94
University of North Carolina 89, 99
University of Northern Colorado 97
University of Oklahoma Press 55, 107
University of Saskatchewan 88
University of South Dakota..........................98
University of Utah 92
University of Washington 87

University of Wisconsin................................86
Ursa major 53

Valoyce-Sanchez, Georgiana.........................50
values 59, 77
Van Camp, Richard 19, 24, 100
Van Wright, Cornelius 19, 100
Vanas, D. J...77, 100
Vann, George 42, 100
Varez, Dietrich 36, 100
Various Indian Peoples 42, 44, 46, 107
Velarde, Pablita 38, 101
Velie, Alan R. 55, 56
Vermont 9, 86
Viborita de cascabel 28
Vickers, Roy Henry.......................................51
Video Librarian..47
Vigil, Felix 34, 101
Viking 57
Virginia (state)..22, 99
Virginia Young Reader (list) 22
Visions of the Buffalo People 78
Visit Teepee Town 57
Vizenor, Gerald 7, 56
Voices of the Rainbow 57
Vojtech, Anna 31, 101
VOYA...21, 61, 68

W. W. Norton 56
Waboose, Jan Bourdeau 19, 23, 101
Waheenee 78
*Walapai..28
Wales, Johnny 30, 101
Walker & Co. 11, 40, 107
Wallis, Velma 27
Walters, Anna Lee 7, 56, 73, 101
Walters, Blackhawk.......................................48
*Wampanoag 23, 28, 32, 62, 96, 102
wampum belts 78
Wampum Belts of the Iroquois 78
*Warm Springs 50
Warren, Charles 59
Warren, W. W. 78
*Washo 62
Washo baskets 62
Waterlily 7
Waterman, Carson.................................11, 101
Watkins, Sherrin 15, 25, 101
Watling, James..8, 101
Way, Diane 41
We Are Still Here series 61-64, 67, 75-76, 78
We Rode the Wind..78
weaving 14, 76, 78-79, 102

Weaving a California Tradition 78, 102	Wood, Carol 82
Weber, Marion 41	Wood, Colleen 17, 102
Weis, Dawn..82	Wood, Karenne 51
Welborn, Lynda 82	Woodland Indians 40
Welburn, Ron 51	Woodruff, Joan Leslie 7
Welch, James 7	Woody, Elizabeth 7, 51
West Indies...19	*Wopila* 48
WestWinds Press 30, 104, 107	*Words of Wisdom for Children* 79
What's the Most Beautiful......................24, 100	Worn Staff, Sadie 41
When Hopi Children... ....40, 88, 99, 102	*Wyandot 97
When the Chenoo Howls 40	*Wynema* 7
When the Moon Is Full............................54, 86	Wyoming Indian Paintbrush (list) 22
When the Rain Sings 55	
When Thunders Spoke 24	Yamane, Linda 27, 78, 102
Whipple, Catherine 75, 101	*Yankton..49
White, Neal..59	*Yaqui 15, 18, 79, 95-96
White Bead Ceremony.....................................25	*Yaqui Coloring Book*..79
White Deer of Autumn 10, 14, 71, 102	Yava, Aaron 57
White Pine Press 57	Yazzie, Rhiana 41
Whiteman, Roberta Hill 51	Yellow Moon Press 43, 45, 48, 107
Whitethorne, Baje 13, 24, 102	Yellow Robe, William S. 41
Whitewolf, J. (Jim) 78	Yerxa, Leo...53, 102
Who Speaks for Wolf 47, 91	Young, Ed..39, 102
Wild Harvest 7	Young, Judy Dockrey 56
Wildcat, Daniel R. 83	Young, Richard 56
William, Gerry 7	Young, Stella 83
William Allen White Award.....................9, 15	Young Bear, Ray..51
Williams, Maria 34, 102	*Young Native Americans Today* 70
Williams, Ted 7	Young-Ing, Greg..51
Williston, Ralph 50	youth....................21, 52-53, 55, 65, 77, 83, 92
Wilson, Darryl Babe......................................59	youth's writings 53, 55
Wilson, Mary Louise Defender 43, 45, 102	Youyouseyah 40, 102
Wilson, Terry P. 83	Yukon..94
The Window 25	*Yuma..66
The Wing 25	
*Winnebago 64	Zaffran, Barbara 83
Winnemucca, (Hopkins) Sarah....................59	Zepeda, Ofelia 51
winter 9, 35, 45, 53, 57, 83	*A Zia Book* 21
Winter White and Summer Gold 83	Zitkala-Sa...55
Witt, Shirley Hill 7	*Zuni 39, 46, 69, 83
Wittstock, Laura Waterman 67, 102	*Zuñi..29
Wolfhouse Publishing 30, 107	*Zuni Children and Elders...* 69
women 32, 45, 56-57, 60, 62, 70, 74, 83, 87, 95, 99, 101-102